Brian and Eileen Anderson

# walk & eat NORTH CYPRUS

# CONTENTS

If holidays are about new experiences then this pocket guide will add a further dimension to your stay in Northern Cyprus. It solves two problems, where to walk and where to find some good, traditional food. The gastronomical touch extends a little further with recipes for some of the island's regional dishes, both specialities and traditional. There are strolls for those who want them or longer walks if those are preferred. If it's just some recommendations for where to eat, look no further. The highlights at a glance:

- 11 day walks, each with topographical map
- 4 fairly long excursions — all car tours
- recommended restaurants for all walks and excursions
- recipes to make at your self-catering base or back home
- hints on finding wheat-, gluten- and dairy-free foods

# INTRO

# THE WALKS

Our walks vary in length and difficulty. None is too strenuous, and all can be done by a reasonably fit walker. They are spread across the region and there is at least one near every major resort. The bus service in North Cyprus relies entirely on mini-buses called *dolmuş.* Major villages enjoy a regular service, but these are mainly coastal so they are not especially useful for our walks — so a hire car is the best option.

# THE EXCURSIONS

Four excursions are featured, covering much of the island's north. A first goes to famous Famagusta (Gazimağusa) in the east. The second heads in the opposite direction — to Vouni and Soli in the west; en route we pass near to Cape Koruçam, from where our recommended walks fan out

## North Cyprus today

After the division of the island by military intervention in 1974, the Turkish population was confined to the north and the Greeks to the south. These two communities are divided by the United Nations controlled Green Line. This military intervention lead to the international isolation of the northern sector, now called the Turkish Republic of North Cyprus.

The high tensions of the early years have subsided, and more recent history is punctuated with talks to find a way to bring unity to this beautiful island. Each failure brings them a step closer, and each new initiative at talks brings new hope. Peace has settled over the whole island, and both the Turkish north and the Greek south are safe and rewarding holiday destinations.

Turks born and bred on Cyprus regard themselves as Turkish Cypriots, which distinguishes them from Turks brought in from Turkey to boost the population after 1974. We have been careful to use this term throughout the book.

east. The third excursion takes in the ridge road on the Kyrenia mountain range, where we visit St Hilarion Castle. Finally, we head to the far northeastern 'panhandle', the Karpaz Peninsula, where the last of our countryside walks is based.

All the excursions are *car tours;* unlike most destinations in the 'walk & eat' series, there is no public transport to take you easily to these out-of-the way highlights.

## Driving tips

Cars drive on the left, just as in the UK. The standard of driving is less disciplined, but seems to follow a pattern. Nobody expects to wait more than a moment at a road junction, and motorists are quick to push into the main stream of traffic.

You must carry your driving licence and car hire documents for any police check.

Unfortunately, the British disease of speed cameras has infected North Cyprus, and there are many of them. They *do work,* and the fines are significant. Should you be clocked by one, the fine will be sent about a month later to the car hire company (who will identify you). You may well have returned home by then, but that is not the end of the story. The offence will be logged on the computer alongside your passport number awaiting your next visit.

# THE CAFÉS AND RESTAURANTS

We only feature places where we have eaten ourselves and which meet our main criterion: those serving good, traditional North Cypriot dishes using fresh ingredients. (A second guideline is that the establishment must be conveniently located for the associated walk.) Thus we have omitted all 'international' and other ethnic restaurants, no matter how good — and there are many!

Apart from restaurants, there are two other types of place to eat in North Cyprus, the kebab house and the *pide salonu.*

A kebab house very often has fixed prices and no menu. The food consists of many (sometimes dozens of) small *meze* dishes, followed eventually by kebabs — which may be a choice of chicken or lamb, or you may simply get both! Go with a good appetite, for we have yet to visit a kebab house where we could finish all the food offered.

The traditional *pide salonu* offers good healthy fast food, Turkish Cypriot style, at exceptionally low prices. Unfortunately, these are mostly located in towns and larger villages, so we have only been able to mention one in our walks. When out and about in Kyrenia or Famagusta, these are worth considering for a lighter lunch or for a picnic take-away *(paket servisi).* More information on the food

## Price guide

Restaurants aren't graded, classified or subject to price controls. As always, there are a few establishments offering a higher standard, where you can expect to pay a little more. For the rest, prices are surprisingly similar. In general terms, it's much cheaper eating in North Cyprus than at home.

The price given in this book (£ to £££) indicates 'very reasonable' to 'fairly pricey'. Remember this guide relates *not* to prices at home, but to North Cyprus, and is a comparison between the various restaurants. The majority fall into the average category indicated by ££. Even so, it's always possible to enjoy a relatively inexpensive meal in a top restaurant by choosing carefully from the menu. There's usually a large choice of inexpensive starter dishes which can easily make up a satisfying meal.

available from a *pide salonu* is given in 'North Cypriot Cuisine' opposite.

## THE RECIPES

Requests for recipes always brought a delighted and enthusiastic response from our hosts. Then the difficulties start. Take a handful of this and a cup of that or take 12 eggs and so on. Weights and measures are not the order of the day. But it was interesting gaining an insight into their preferred herbs. Traditional recipes passed down through the family use only local herbs which grow naturally (or are grown commercially) on the island. Chief of these is parsley, which is used in so many recipes as a flavouring or as decoration. Mint, too, is well used, while oregano, dill and cumin often feature.

Many standard recipes vary quite considerably. Mousaka is a prime example. Each one we tried and each recipe we acquired was so very different. In North Cyprus you can enjoy mousaka with aubergine and potato or with potato and no aubergine or with aubergine and no potato, all with or without béchamel topping!

We learned two tips about cooking dried beans. The first: after soaking, bring to the boil, drain, and boil *again* in fresh water (helps reduce flatulence). Second: to keep the skins tender, add olive oil and salt five minutes before the end of cooking.

So we have drawn all our information together and tried to make the dishes at home to recapture the taste and flavour. It's difficult without exactly the same ingredients, and doubly difficult without the intangibles — the sunshine and holiday atmosphere. Even so, these recipes are authentic and the results pleasing. By the way, olive oil isn't good for frying at high temperatures; the lighter sunflower oil or similar is more commonly used. If you're cooking at home, rapeseed oil is as healthy as olive oil and better for frying.

Smoked salmon salad at Green Heights, one of our favourite restaurants

## NORTH CYPRIOT CUISINE

Travellers in love with Turkish cuisine will find enough to keep them happy in North Cyprus and have some new dishes and flavours to savour. The Greek influence is less than might be expected, and there is a Middle Eastern influence in the use of flavours and spices. Vinegar is sometimes a 'hidden' ingredient in meat and fish dishes, to add a touch of sharpness.

If one dish remains universally popular throughout the island it is *kleftiko.* The word means 'stolen'. In the past, when meat was expensive and hard to come by, it was not unheard of for a lamb or a sheep to be stolen from a flock at night. To avoid detection, the thieves would cook the meat in a large earthenware pot, in an oven made in a hollow in the ground and sealed over. The meat would be marinated in red wine, flavoured with bay leaves and sprinkled with salt and would then be cooked gently for many hours. The modern method is to wrap the dish in a foil parcel and cook slowly in a wood oven. *Kleftiko* (a Greek word) often appears on menus in the north, but watch too for *küp kebapı* — the Turkish term for the same dish.

Peppers (*biber*) are commonly used in the north — and not always the familiar bell peppers. *Sivri biber* is a longish, fairly thin green pepper, and this can be totally sweet or gently hot and is often served on top of something grilled. *Çarliston biber* is a light green, tapering pepper but fairly fat and is totally sweet. The peppers to watch out for are the red or green mouth-numbing chilli peppers, *acı biber*.

There is no disguising the British influence either, with traditional good-value Sunday lunches offered by many restaurants — and not just those run by ex-pats. Sunday lunches are commonly served in the evening throughout the hot summer months.

## THE RESTAURANT MENU *(YEMEK LİSTESİ)*

Starters are usually the first listing, but after that the main courses are often grouped as meat, chicken and fish dishes, perhaps with traditional dishes listed separately.

**Starters** are dominated by ***meze,*** a selection of small dishes, both hot and cold. Most of the dishes listed opposite are perennial favourites, with the exception of *gabbar* and *mangalo,* which only turn up in the spring. The most inventive dish we encountered was a mix of peas with small cubes of apple, some celery and a shrimp or two all bound with yoghurt. *Meze* is

## Typical *meze* dishes

*cacık:* yoghurt dip with cucumber, garlic & mint
*ciğer:* fried liver chopped into small pieces
*çoban salatası:* simple chopped salad
*dolma:* usually a mince/rice mix wrapped in a vine leaf *(yaprak)*, sometimes without meat
*gabbar:* pickled wild caper
*helim (haloumi):* traditional Cypriot cheese, often fried or grilled
*humus:* chick pea in sesame seed paste
*kalamar:* squid
*kısır:* bulgar salad
*köfte:* meat balls
*mangalo:* tender basal leaves and stalks of *Eryngium creticum* as a vegetable in spring
*mercimek koftesi:* bulgar wheat and lentil croquettes
*palluz:* like turnip, partially cooked, cut in fingers, topped with grated cheese
*pancar:* beetroot
*peynir:* white cheese sometimes sprinkled with fresh mint
*piyaz:* white bean salad
*rus salatası:* Russian salad (traditional)
*sarımsaklı yoğurtlu havuç sote:* sautéed carrot/yoghurt salad
*sigara böreği:* usually cheese wrapped in börek (filo pastry) shaped like a cigar
*tahini:* ground sesame seeds
*turşu:* pickle, usually cauliflower but it could be any vegetable.
*zeytin ezmesi:* olive paste
*siyah zeytin ezmesi:* black olive paste
*zeytinyağlı börülce:* black-eyed bean salad

something at which the Turkish Cypriots really excel, full of imagination and invention. Some restaurants, like our featured Tervetuloa in Alsancak, offer six free starters which magically become about 12 if there are two dining! The kebab houses, mentioned above, include a good selection of *meze* as part of the meal. **Soups**, too, often appear on the starters list. If you enjoy **Cyprus potatoes** at home, they are even better on Cyprus, and it is not unusual to get pieces of baked potato amongst the starters.

Amongst the **main courses**, **grills** feature regularly, simply because they can be cooked to order and, unlike prepared dishes, there is no waste on a quiet evening. Beef chops and steaks, lamb or goat, chicken and fish are ever present — and pork chops in some restaurants. Chicken is very popular and cheap, so there is often a good selection of dishes. Any of these **meats** or fish could be offered as a *kebap* or *şiş kebap (*where the meat is interlaced with tomatoes, onions or other vegetables). Turkey is rarely seen on menus.

Smaller restaurants do not regularly offer as many traditional dishes like *kleftiko* or *küp kebapı* (see above), except at weekends, but they feature regularly in larger establishments. Many smaller places say they will make anything you would like if you let them know in advance. Where this is the case with our featured restaurants, we mention it with a telephone number.

Other **Cypriot specialities** include *şheftali,* like a skinless sausage, and the ever-present *köfte,* meatballs. Always made from fresh mince, *köfte* can taste very different according to the spices used. There is a vegetarian equivalent made from bulgar wheat. A real Turkish speciality which remains popular is *imam bayıldı*, meaning 'the imam fainted' — with delight of course! In the original of this dish, there is no mince. An aubergine shoe, cut from half a long aubergine, is filled with diced tomatoes, onions, garlic, parsley etc. and cooked until tender. *Karnıyarık* is a version with mince, although this is sometimes presented as *imam bayıldı*. *Mousaka* has a long claim to fame, the Turks claim ownership, as do the Greeks, but its name suggests Arabic origins. North Cyprus, in the middle of all these influences, has produced versions which are totally different and vary greatly from one restaurant to another.

Strangely for a Mediterranean island, **fish** (*balık*) is not available in great variety nor is it very widely eaten. Most restaurants offer one or two fish dishes, usually sea bass (*levrek*) or a version of cod — perhaps on a skewer as *şiş balık*. Specialist fish restaurants do offer a larger selection, usually including salmon, red mullet (*barbun*), sword fish (*kiliç balığı*), sea bream (*çipura*), squid (*kalamar*), cuttlefish (*sipya*), octopus (*ahtapot*) and a few less familiar fish like *mineri*. This latter comes as a steak from a very large fish and is similar to swordfish.

Don't expect too much in the way of **vegetables** with your main course; the *meze* starters take care of these. Chips are the norm, but you may be offered other forms of potato, and rice too is frequently offered (very often the rice is cooked together with shreds of vermicelli pasta). *Molohiya*, a green leafy vegetable which grows only in Cyprus and on the banks of the Nile, is a very unusual speciality. The closest analogy is with spinach, but here it is cooked with chicken or meat. Perhaps not to everyone's taste, try it. Another interesting vegetable, little known outside Cyprus, is *kolokas*, a root vegetable which, when cooked (again with lamb or chicken), has the texture of potato but a sweeter taste.

**Pasta** (*makarna*) dishes are usually fairly simple, some form of pasta covered with a sauce but not always meat, and maybe a cheese sauce or yoghurt topping. The Turks have their own pasta called *manti*, a little like ravioli, which originated in Central Asia. Made fresh it is meat-filled, but normally it is bought dry. A recipe is included in Walk 1 for a traditional dish of *manti* topped with yoghurt and pepper sauce. *Fırın makarna,* mince topped with tubular *makarna* pasta and a white cheese sauce and baked in the oven, is the most popular of the baked pasta dishes. Even this simple dish can vary considerably.

**Vegetarians** will find a selection of suitable dishes on most menus and virtually all the meze starters are vegetarian, and most are suitable for **gluten-free** diets.

The Turkish Cypriots certainly like their **desserts** *(tatlılar)*, and there is quite a selection available. Restaurants mostly have a limited choice, but the supermarkets carry a range of ready-made traditional desserts. Fruit is always popular, so *mesim meyveleri* (seasonal fruit) may be listed or *meyra tabiği* (fruit platter). Another regular is *baklava*, a filo pastry sweet, multi-layered with nuts, baked until golden brown and soaked in syrup. This might be a traditional Turkish sweet, but it is just as popular here as is rice pudding (*sütlaç*). Traditionally this is flavoured with rose water, but not always in North Cyprus.

Less frequently found but still locally appreciated is *kunefe*, a sweet shredded pastry with cheese, and the same is true of *ekmek kadayıfı*, rather like a sweet bread pudding, often served with *kaymak,* Turkish clotted cream. Noah's pudding (*aşure*), said to be made originally by Noah from all the bits of food left in the Ark, contains a mixture of pulses, perhaps with sultanas and apricots or even pomegranate seeds — much loved but not always on the menu. It can be bought in one or two of the supermarkets and is well worth a try. Two more to mention are the Istanbul speciality, *kazandibi,* a caramelised milk pudding, and *keşkül*, an almond milk pudding.

One or two restaurants actually offer a free sweet which is likely to be fruit or perhaps a small piece of *baklava* with a little fruit.

**Coffee**, instant or Turkish, and **brandy** is also very often offered free after a meal. Although this is a Muslim country, the indigenous people are very relaxed about their religion, and alcohol is widely enjoyed. Expect to find a full range of alcohol on the **drinks menu** (*içki listesi* for alcoholic drinks and *meşrubat* for soft drinks). You can have beer to brandy, whisky to wine. Local spirits like gin are both cheap and good, so some diners prefer to drink that through the meal as an alternative to a more expensive wine. *Rakı,* an aniseed-flavoured spirit, taken with ice and water, is favoured by the locals and is a drink to sort the men from the boys.

The wine list is often quite short in most restaurants and usually features Turkey's most popular and very palatable red wines, Yakut and Angora, with the slightly lighter Vila Doluca

**The *lahmacun/pide* restaurant menu**

If you are only looking for a lunchtime snack, these are great places to eat and so inexpensive. You can eat in or ask for a take-away *(paket servisi)*.

*Lahmacun* is like a very thin pizza base covered with an equally thin layer of mince or cheese. It is usual to order more than one and they usually come with a mixed salad. Our particular favourite is a *dürüm*, a wrap of thin *lavaş* bread filled with either chicken or lamb and a little salad. It is usually served with a little dish of hot peppers and a slice of lemon. Just occasionally the meat may be in a pitta envelope instead of a wrap.

There are also the usual *şiş kebabs*, chicken *(tavuk)* or lamb *(kuzu)* and a range of ordinary kebabs like *adana kebap* — mincemeat slid off the skewer. The traditional drink here is a slightly salty yoghurt drink called *ayran* — a great, inexpensive drink for summer and you can buy it anywhere.

*Photograph: Chicken wrap with* ayran

also on offer. Similarly the white list has two leading contenders, Angora and Çamkaya. In larger restaurants there is a fuller wine list including wines from other countries.

The local Efes, a lager-type beer, is very popular and almost certain be on the list, as well as other leading brands.

# PLANNING YOUR VISIT

## How to get there

Since North Cyprus is not yet internationally recognised, it cannot accept direct, non-stop flights. But it is still easy to get there at any time of year. Frequent scheduled flights from the UK to North Cyprus are operated by Turkish Airlines from Manchester, Birmingham, London Heathrow and London Stansted via Istanbul Atatürk airport. Passengers change flights at

Istanbul to continue to Ercan airport in North Cyprus (east of Lefkoşa).

Cyprus Turkish Airlines fly frequent scheduled flights from Manchester, Birmingham and all London airports and, similarly, Pegasus flies from London Stansted. In the case of these airlines, although they land at a Turkish airport possibly to put down and pick up, **passengers do not leave the aircraft and do not change flights**. As a consequence of international restrictions, there are no charter flights to the north.

Since it is now easy to cross from the Greek Cypriot south to the north, flying into the **southern airport of Larnaca** opens up many more options. There are plenty of charter flights in summer but, more importantly for walkers, there are year round scheduled flights. Monarch Airlines offer good value flights from Gatwick, Luton, Birmingham and Manchester; easyJet flies from Gatwick, and Cyprus Airways from Heathrow, Stansted and Manchester. Larnaca is just about an hour's drive from the Metehan Green Line crossing point in Nicosia. You will need to organise transport to get to the crossing point, and it is much cheaper to pre-hire a North Cyprus taxi which will come to meet you at Larnaca. If you pre-hire a car in the north, the car hire company will arrange your transfer; otherwise look on the North Cyprus web forum

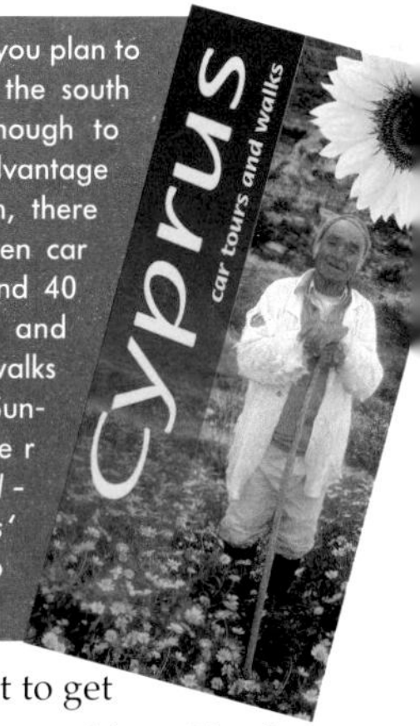


***Tip:*** If you plan to stay in the south long enough to take advantage of them, there are seven car tours and 40 long and short walks in the Sunflower *'Landscapes'* guide to Cyprus.

www.cyprus44. com to find a taxi firm before you travel.

Paphos airport in the south is much further away, and it's still necessary to use the same crossing point in Nicosia.

## When to go

Cyprus is blessed with a very mild winter climate but suffers from heat in the high summer months, especially July and August. Many of the hotels in North Cyprus remain open all through the year, so it is very much a destination for any season.

The **best time for walking** is in the winter, spring and autumn. The winter season is a great time for walking, from November right through to March. You can count on it being cooler (but rarely cold), which makes the mountain walks seem so much easier. Winter rain has been in short supply these last few years; it

## Crossing points in Lefkoşa/ Nicosia

There are three crossing points in Lefkoşa (Nicosia), but only Metehan, to the west of the centre, is a vehicle crossing point. Ledra Palace is a foot crossing with vehicle access, convenient if you are meeting someone crossing on foot with luggage. The Ledra Street (Lokmaci) crossing is another foot crossing point right in the centre of the old town, but without vehicle access. People travelling to Famagusta may prefer the Akyar crossing point on the Larnaca-Famagusta road nearer to Famagusta.

The procedure for crossing the green line is straightforward; you just need your passport. Then, at the North Cypriot passport control, you will need to fill in a slip of paper with your name, nationality and passport number. This will be stamped instead of your passport and is, in effect, a 90-day visa. Keep it with your passport for cancellation on departure.

Doorway in Lefkoşa

can be showery, but there is always sunshine around. There are flowers, too, but not in such great numbers although some of the orchids and the colourful anemones start as early as January.

March, April and May are our favourite months. The temperature isn't too high, and the rich array of spring flowers is a definite bonus. The heat starts to build quickly from the end of May, and at some point it becomes too hot to enjoy strenuous walks — but some of the easy or short walks remain possible, especially with an early start. July, August and early September are generally too hot for walking unless you rise with the sun and walk *very, very early* in the morning. Walking in the full heat of the sun in this period is risking serious heat exhaustion and is *most definitely not recommended.*

Temperatures decline slowly throughout September and usually by the middle of the month, walking is back on the agenda, but it may still be advisable to avoid strenuous walks for a time. By October the temperatures are usually back to the mid or low 20s, and walking becomes a pleasure again.

## Place names

All the towns and villages in the north had their names changed after 1974. For the smaller towns and villages, the Turkish names are well established and are the *only* names used today. On old maps or on Greek maps, the earlier Greek names will be found.

With Kyrenia, Nicosia and Famagusta, the internationally known main towns, the situation is different. Kyrenia became Girne, but both names are used equally. Lefkoşa is more commonly used than Nicosia, but Famagusta remains favoured over Gazimağusa (sometimes the old Byzantine name of Madusa is also used). They are all in common usage, equally recognised and understood.

## Where to stay

Unusually, North Cyprus has no recognised 'resorts'. It comes down to a choice whether to stay somewhere around centrally sited **Kyrenia** or way out to the east in or near **Famagusta**. If your holidays are all about beaches, then Famagusta might be the right choice, but for walkers it has to be Kyrenia which is so close to the mountains.

Most of the accommodation in the north is scattered around the Kyrenia area. There are top-quality hotels in the town itself and outside. Surprisingly, there are few three-star hotels, but **holiday villages** offer a different choice. A holiday village

Kyrenia (Girne) harbour

typically has houses or bungalows set in extensive gardens and with one or more swimming pools. A lot of this type of accommodation is found out to the west, on the way to Alsancak and Lapta.

## What to take

There is no special dress code for dining, except that shorts are not always appreciated in restaurants and some tavernas during the evening. It's more important to concentrate on packing suitable walking gear.

**Walking boots** are the footwear we most strongly recommend, but not all the walks demand them. Some of the track walks are fairly easy underfoot, and for those **walking shoes** or specialist walking **trainers** are sufficient. Each person should carry a small **rucksack**, and it's advisable to pack it with a **sunhat**, **suncream** and some extra **warm clothing**. A **long-sleeved shirt** and **long trousers** should be worn or carried for sun protection and for walking through spiny vegetation. You should always carry a **mobile 'phone**; the **emergency numbers** in North Cyprus are **112** (health, ambulance) and **155** (police). If you plan to use your mobile to make local calls, it pays to buy a pay-as-you-go sim card. They are inexpensive from a 'phone shop and they will check to make sure it works in your phone.

Depending on the season, you may also need lightweight **rainwear** and a lightweight **folding umbrella**. The umbrella can also be useful for sun protection on open sections of the walks. A reliable litre-size **water bottle** is well worth packing, although small, easy-to-carry bottles of water can be bought almost everywhere. ***It's imperative that each walker carries at least a half-litre of water and a full litre or more when the weather is hot.***

## Planning your walks

The Kyrenia range, known as the **Five Finger *(Beşparmak)* Mountains**, is a wonderful range of craggy limestone running roughly parallel with the coast. It rises in the west before Karşıyaka and runs east for around 100km (62 miles), before petering out to the east of Kantara Castle. The range takes its name from one particular peak, lying east of Kyrenia, which is shaped like five very stubby fingers (five knuckles might be better — as you can see in the photograph on page 96). Our Walk 6 circles the Five Fingers peak. The highest peak in the range, near Lapta in the west, rises to 1024m (3360ft). The whole range is a wonderful playground for walkers and offers walks to suit all grades.

Look over your selected walks in advance, to check out the **transport** requirements. There may be a walk or two on your doorstep and, depending where you stay, one or two more may be reached by public transport, but the rest will require a hire car or taxi.

We have **graded the walks** with the weekend walker in mind and *based on ambient temperatures below the mid 20s C.* When the temperatures rise above this level, walkers expend more energy in simply keeping cool, and uphill walking especially is much more tiring. When the temperatures are on the high side, the suggested grade will be at least half a grade higher. The walking times work out at around 3-4km/hour, but more slowly uphill. This is easily within the scope of casual walkers, **but remember: they are neat walking times** and take no account of any stops.

**Walking safely** depends on knowing what to expect and being properly equipped. For this reason we urge you to *read through the whole walk description* at your leisure before setting out so you have a mental picture of each stage of the route and of landmarks.

**Thunderstorms** in late autumn, after a long summer

drought, can cause serious **flash flooding**, posing severe danger to walkers. Keep an eye on the forecast at this time of the year and do not take risks with the weather.

# ON ARRIVAL

## Tourist information & maps

Tourist Information offices are located by the old harbour in Kyrenia/Girne, by the Land Gate (the main entrance to Famagusta old town), and by Kyrenia Gate in Nicosia/Lefkoşa. Local town maps are available in these offices and, in Lefkoşa, remember to pick up a 'Nicosia Trail' map which describes highlights on our featured Walk 11.

The best general map is the 1:250,00 map *Rough Guide Map to Cyprus,* which shows both Turkish and Greek names for the northern towns and villages. It is best to buy it before travelling. There are plenty of maps on sale locally which are just about adequate.

## Transport

Mini-buses, *dolmuş*, provide the public transport system between the main towns and the villages. There are no timetables, but generally they are very frequent and inexpensive. Outside towns you can pick them up anywhere by flagging them down. (Sometimes, when you're walking along a *dolmuş* route, a passing bus will slow down in the hope of picking up a passenger or two.) But the routes ply between centres of population and not into the countryside, so they are only useful on our Walk 3.

## Shopping for self-catering

Self-catering accommodation as such is rarely seen advertised in North Cyprus, but some holiday village accommodation does provide adequate self-catering facilities. Even so, few people want to waste warm evenings cooking when they could be out enjoying the atmosphere. Just now and again it is appealing to enjoy a meal on your own balcony, and there are one or two meals which can be assembled quickly without toiling in the heat.

Salads are easy enough to put together, and most supermarkets have a **salad bar counter**, where you can buy a whole range of ready-made dishes to make a complete meal. A selection typically includes *çoban salatası*, a simple mixed salad of lettuce, tomatoes, olives and cucumber all chopped together, *humus*, *cacık* (a yoghurt and cucumber mix), beetroot, *kısır* (a bulgar wheat salad with onions), and maybe one or two bean salads. These are sold by weight

Supermarket shopping list reminder

bread
butter
coffee/tea/drinking chocolate
eggs
garlic paste (1tsp for one clove)
herbs & spices
juice
mayonnaise/mustard/sauce
milk (long life or fresh)
mineral water
olive oil soap (excellent for removing stubborn marks when hand washing)
olive oil (salads) & vinegar
paper towels and/or napkins
rice/pasta
salt & pepper
scouring pads
soap
sugar
Sunflower oil (cooking)
tissues
tomato purée
washing up liquid
washing powder for hand washing (look for the hand wash logo on the box).
wine/beer/rakı

in a clear plastic box. Ask for the size of box you require, small (*küçük*), medium (*orta*) or large (*büyük*). You can always stop them while they are filling the box with a quick OK (*tamam*). **Spit-roast chicken** is almost always available, which is a good complement to salad. Some supermarkets have a **hot counter** selling ready-made dishes — chops, lamb, meatballs and maybe a Turkish dish or two.

Most supermarkets have a **vegetable counter** of some kind. The larger supermarkets and the local outdoor markets offer a better choice of fresh vegetables. Lettuce, tomatoes, onions, cucumbers and peppers are the basics stocked by most supermarkets. Remember these are often **local produce** and are not treated or chemically sprayed in any way to make them look or stay fresh, except with water.

The **delicatessen counter** is where you can buy your **cheese** too. There is a wide selection available, but the local and most popular cheese is *beyaz peynir*, white cheese. This is normally an unsalted cheese made from sheep, cow or goats milk — or even a mix. Although unsalted, the outside is patted with salt for protection. This same cheese is used to make the famous *helim* (*haloumi*) which is a salted cheese. *Helim* is a slightly rubbery cheese which tends to squeak on your teeth but is very popular for grilling and is often served that way as a *meze*.

**Meat** and **fish** can be bought from the big supermarkets; beef, lamb and chicken are common, but turkey is rare. Ready-made kebabs are sometimes available, or the butcher will cut the meat into suitably sized pieces if you mention '*şiş*'. Fish counters are somewhat disappointing, with a relatively poor selection, and many of the fish on offer will not be familiar.

**Vegetarians**, **vegans** and **lactose intolerant** people should have no problem finding what they need, and soya milk products are commonly sold in supermarkets. **Gluten-free** food is much harder to find; although rice cakes are sometimes sold in larger supermarkets, it is best to bring your g-f needs with you. (However, before you travel, look on the North Cyprus forum, www.cyprus44.com, which had some helpful information about gluten-free flours, etc, at press date and will no doubt herald the arrival of any international g-f products.)

## Fruit and veg market

Wednesday is market day in Kyrenia. It is a popular venue for buying everything from clothing to household goods, but especially good for fresh fruit and veg. The market lies on the west side of town, off the road to Alsancak and Lapta. Turn left just before the water fountain roundabout, to find it a few hundred yards further along on the right, by the bus station. The market stalls cover a fairly extensive area, and there is a huge choice of fresh fruit and vegetables.

Mixed peppers in the market

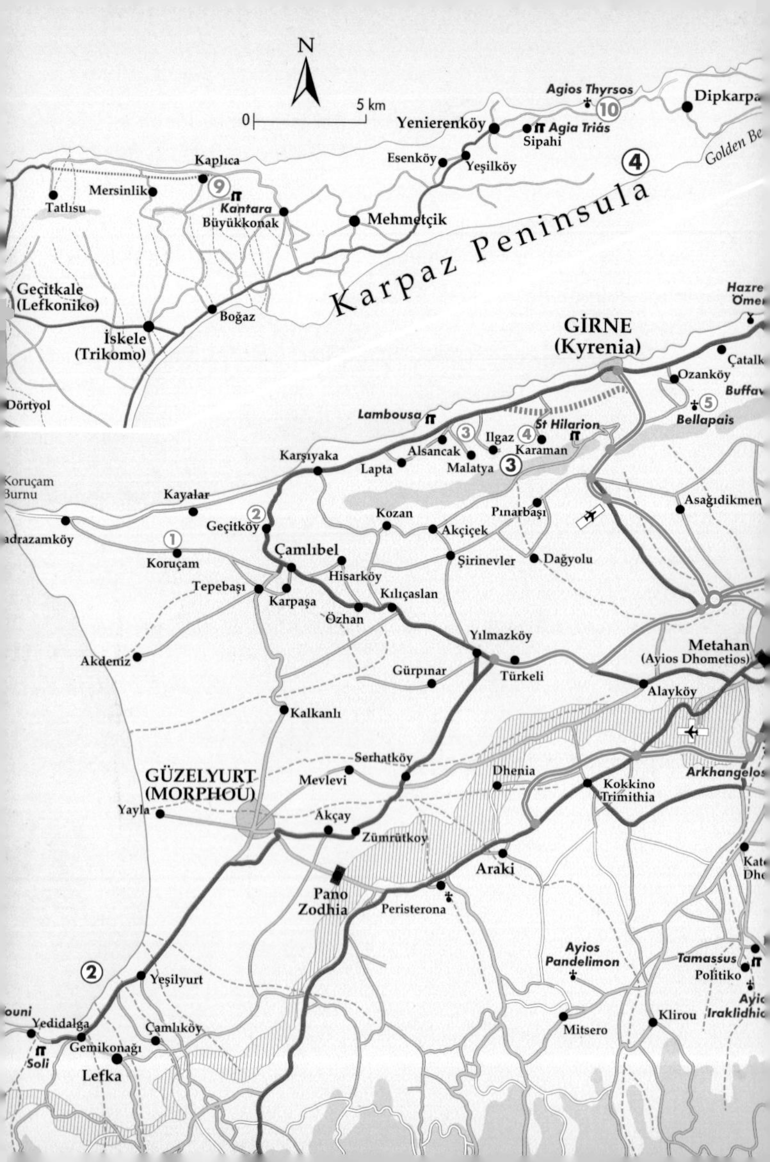

N
0
5 km
Karpaz Peninsula
Agios Thyrsos
Dipkarpa
Yenierenköy
Agia Triás
Sipahi
Golden Be
Esenköy
Yeşilköy
Kaplıca
Mersinlik
Tatlısu
Kantara
Büyükkonak
Mehmetçik
Geçitkale (Lefkoniko)
Boğaz
İskele (Trikomo)
Dörtyol
Hazre Ömer
GİRNE (Kyrenia)
Çatalk
Ozanköy
Buffav
Bellapais
Lambousa
St Hilarion
Ilgaz
Karaman
Alsancak
Malatya
Lapta
Karşıyaka
Koruçam Burnu
Kayalar
Geçitköy
adrazamköy
Koruçam
Kozan
Akçiçek
Pınarbaşı
Asağıdikmen
Çamlıbel
Hisarköy
Şirinevler
Dağyolu
Tepebaşı
Karpaşa
Kılıçaslan
Özhan
Yılmazköy
Akdeniz
Türkeli
Gürpınar
Metahan (Ayios Dhometios)
Alayköy
Kalkanlı
Serhatköy
Mevlevi
Dhenia
Kokkino Trimithia
Arkhangelos
GÜZELYURT (MORPHOU)
Yayla
Akçay
Zümrütkoy
Araki
Pano Zodhia
Peristerona
Kat Dh
Ayios Pandelimon
Tamassus
Politiko
Ayio Iraklidhio
Yeşilyurt
ouni
Yedidalga
Soli
Gemikonağı
Çamlıköy
Lefka
Mitsero
Klirou

Zafer Burnu
Boğaz
Tatlısu
Ağıllar
Altınova
Bahçeler
İskele (Trikomo)
Çınarlı
Sınırüstü
Esentepe (Ayios Amvrosios)
Yamaçköy
Antiphonitis
Akova
Kuzucuk
Karaağaç
Çamlıca
Geçitkale (Lefkoniko)
Yıldırım
Salamis
Aloda
Gönendere
Sütlüce
Alaniçi
St Barnabas
Gömeç
Alevkaya Forest Station
Egkomi Alasia
Mutluyaka
Pınarlı
Nergizli
Serdarlı
Kalavaç
Dörtyol
Pirhan
Korkuteli
GAZİMAĞUSA (Famagusta)
Ulukışla
Değirmenlik (Kythrea)
Ayios Nikolaos
İnönü
Meriç
Gaziköy
Paşaköy
Vadili
Köprülü
Akdoğan (Lysi)
İncirli
Düzce (Athna)
Avgorou
LEFKOŞA (Nicosia)
Ercan
Yiğitler
Dilekkaya
Erdemli
Xylotimbou
Kırıkkale
La Cava
Pyla
A3
Kiracıköy (Atheniou)
Trouli
Dhekelia
Gaziler
Laxia
Potamia
Idalium
Livadhia
A1
Lourojina
Dhali
A3
10 km
6 mi
Lymbia
A2
A2
LARNAKA (Larnaca)
Ayia Varvara
Lythrodhonda
area of the walk
area of the excursion
prohibited military area
'Green Line' buffer zone and crossing points

Historic Famagusta (Gazimağusa), encapsulated within its old Venetian walls, is a world apart from the modern, noisy, energetic Famagusta lying outside. The very early origins of this city are not as obvious as the next stop on this excursion, Salamis, where you are cast back through the centuries.

# 1 famagusta and salamis EXCURSION

**Distance:** about 160km/100mi; allow a full day's driving from and back to Kyrenia and plenty of time to visit Famagusta and Salamis. Be sure, too, to carry at least ample drinking water for the Salamis visit (*no* refreshments in the site itself).

**Route:** Kyrenia — Lefkoşa — Famagusta — Salamis — St Barnabas — Mutluyaka — Dörtyol — Geçitkale — Kyrenia

**Refreshments:** Petek Pastahanesi (patisserie/coffee shop) and Aspava in Famagusta; Bedis by the entrance to Salamis; Kocareis north of Salamis

There is a choice of three routes from Kyrenia to Famagusta, so this excursion heads out by one route and returns by another. **From Kyrenia** take the road to Lefkoşa which climbs over the Kyrenia Mountains, passing the road off to St Hilarion Castle. On dropping down to the plain, turn left at the large roundabout on the **outskirts of Lefkoşa**, following signs for Famagusta (a fast road laced with speed cameras). When you see the old walls of **Famagusta**, head right, keeping the walls on your left, and continue round towards the port. Turn left immediately, to enter the gate nearest the coast and find somewhere to park. There are car parks inside the gate, and finding space is not usually a problem.

Once inside the open-air museum of old Famagusta, the ghostly Gothic ruins stimulate the imagination to run riot over past events. The history of Famagusta, telling of its growth from a minor Byzantine fishing port to one of the richest and most important cities of the late Middle Ages, is fascinating. For more detail ask in the tourist office in Kyrenia or Famagusta (at the Land Gate) for the 'Walking Tour map of Famagusta'. This gives an excellent history from ancient to modern.

From wherever you park, head first to the **Lion Statue** near the **Sea Gate** (around the middle of the seaward wall). If you want to stretch your legs straight away, you can climb the steps on the Venetian wall nearby to the top of the bastion for a great view of the city and harbour. Nearby is **Othello's Tower** (small entry charge); just continue with the walls on your right, to reach it in a couple of minutes — it's the southwest corner

The open-air museum of old Famagusta

tower of a medieval fortress now enclosed within the town walls. It got its name during the British period, from Shakespeare's tragic hero, a 16th-century Venetian captain stationed in a Cyprus sea port. This fortress is actually the oldest surviving Lusignan building in Famagusta and contains a central court with five high vaulted chambers that make up the great hall. Again you can climb to the upper levels of the battlements to gain extensive views.

Continue down Limanyolu Street to reach **Namik Kemal Square** and the most iconic monument in Famagusta, the **cathedral of St Nicholas** (now **Lala Mustafa Paşa Mosque**). The French Crusader Guy de Lusignan, a Roman Catholic, bought the island of Cyprus in 1192 and established the Lusignan Kingdom which survived until 1489. With the fall of the major Middle Eastern port of Acre in 1291, Famagusta became an even more active and profitable trading centre as immigrants flooded the town with new capital, so that by the 14th century it was thought to be the world's richest city. Traders and merchants from dozens of Mediterranean ports, all the major European players, were there. Even though the Middle East was controlled by the Muslims, trade did not cease, and now the lion's share of the goods passed through Famagusta.

The cathedral's construction began around 1300, and it was consecrated in 1328. This is where the Lusignans were to be crowned Kings of Jerusalem, so the cathedral had to be a fitting place. The more decorated style of Gothic architecture developing in France was followed here, and the result was a cathedral almost the twin of the one in the French town of Rheims. The upper parts of the mosque's two towers were badly damaged during the Ottoman bombardments of 1571 and never repaired. With the Ottomans now in control, the cathedral was converted to a mosque. Visitors can enter, provided no religious services are taking place (small charge).

St Nicholas Cathedral — now the Lala Mustafa Paşa Mosque

The cathedral is not the only thing standing from the 14th century, the tree by the main door, an African fig, *Ficus sycomorus*, with leaves like a mulberry tree, is said to have been planted at the same time.

The robust wall with three splendid arches on the opposite corner of the square is the façade of a **Venetian Palace**. It was originally the royal palace of the Lusignans, but when the Venetians arrived it became the official residence of the acting governor. Modifications in the late 15th century transformed its original Gothic features into the solid Italian Renaissance style. The four columns on the façade are from Salamis.

Leave the cathedral bearing slightly left, to enter pedestrianised **Istiklal Avenue** and run the gauntlet of tourist shops and cafés. The large church ruins you might have glimpsed over to the right are the remains of the church of **St Peter and St Paul** — one of the finest and best-preserved Gothic churches in Famagusta. Continue to the end of the avenue, to find the great bastion of the **Land Gate** (small entry charge). This is where the **Tourist Office** is housed With all its secret passages, it offers a rare opportunity to see some extraordinary medieval military architecture. This gate was one of two original entrances to the old town. It is a complex of enormously thick walls (8m/26ft in places), galleries and dry moats. During the Ottoman siege of 1571, it took almost a year to capture Famagusta, but this bastion survived remarkably well.

Salamis: the Gymnasium

After perhaps having lunch (see page 37), leave Famagusta by heading north, and follow signs to the ancient site of **Salamis**. There is a free car park, but of course a charge to enter the site (this includes a leaflet with a plan, some history, and a description of the major ruins). Salamis, the most important ancient site on Cyprus, covers a huge area. Wandering through the standing **columns** and exploring the **ancient theatre**, you are cast back to the 12th century BC. But remember that if you are intent on seeing all the major features, including the **Kampanopetra basilica** by the edge of the sea and the inland **Roman agora**, then you can expect to walk some 4km/2.5mi —much more if you take any wrong turns (which

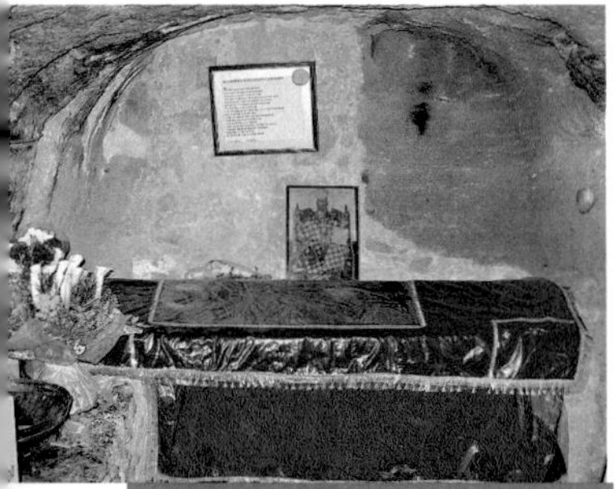
The Tomb of St Barnabas

we have done a number of times).

Leave Salamis by turning left at the main road, initially heading back towards Famagusta. Very shortly, take the road off right signposted to **St Barnabas**. You can wander about freely in the **monastery cloisters**, but there is a small charge to enter the **Icon and Archaeological Museum**. Barnabas was the companion of the Apostle Paul and was influential in introducing Christianity to the island. The present monastery building was constructed around 1756. The **Tomb of St Barnabas** is a short walk away from the front of the monastery, near the eucalyptus trees (beware the uneven steps leading down to the tomb).

Rejoin the road to return: turn right and drive through **Mutluyaka** to join the Famagusta/Lefkoşa road. Head towards Lefkoşa, but only for a short way: at **Dörtyol** turn right for Geçitkale. At the **crossroads on the edge of Geçitkale**, turn right again, but again only for a short distance, then turn left just before a garage on the corner. This leads into a new road which runs over a low pass to the north coast. Be aware that there is a short stretch along the route which is still unsurfaced (ownership dispute!) and there are some slight changes of level without warning, Turn left at the junction when you reach the coast road and continue back to **Kyrenia** following signs.

As always in touristic places like Famagusta old town, the restaurants don't seem to try very hard, since they are not aiming to attract long-term customers. We found **Aspava** on Limanyolu Street acceptable for a meal, but there is another opportunity to dine at **Bedis Restaurant** by the entrance to Salamis. **Kocareis Restaurant** at the edge of the sea a little further north from Salamis is another choice (turn right for the Mimosa Hotel to it).

Bedis Restaurant at the entrance to Salamis (right), and a chocolate treat from Petek Pastahanesi

But *don't miss* **Petek Pastahanesi**, the patisserie/coffee shop on the corner of Limanyolu Street in Famagusta, almost opposite the Lion Statue. It's worth going in just to see their mouth-watering selection of cakes. You can buy cakes from the shop to take away, or order your cake, wander through to the coffee shop area and have it with a drink.

# 2

Soli and Vouni, two ancient sites, lie in the far west: to get there, you cross the largest orange-growing region in the north and traverse an old copper mining region. There is little tourism out here, so the towns and villages are very traditional – you might see men in Lefke wearing turbans.

## western civilisations

# EXCURSION

**Distance:** about 160km/100mi; allow a full day — to visit both sites, stop at Güzelyurt and wander around Lefke.

**Route:** Kyrenia — Alsancak — Geçitköy — Güzelyurt — Lefke — Soli— Vouni — Kyrenia

**Refreshments:** Aspava and King Fish restaurants at Yedidalga, between Soli and Vouni

**Leave Kyrenia** by taking the road out west towards Alsancak and Lapta. The traffic usually melts away once past **Alsancak** but, if you are inclined to pick up speed, take heed of the speed camera warning signs, there has been a heavy investment in cameras along the whole of this route. Drive through **Geçitköy** (Walk 2 starts nearby) and climb over the low pass, to head inland. Take the right turn by the petrol station (signposted Güzelyurt). The road continues through light pine woods to **Kalkanlı**, then starts to descend from a ridge. A view opens up over the extensive plain surrounding Güzelyurt, effectively a huge orange grove.

Very soon you are driving amongst the orange trees, as you head into the sprawling market town of **Güzelyurt**. Keep right on entering the town, following signs to Lefke. This brings you almost immediately to the museum and the church of Agias Mamas, which are perhaps the only reasons for stopping. There is a small charge to enter the **Natural History and**

Güzelyurt Museum

**Agias Mamas**
Legend has it that Mamas was a 12th century saint who lived in a cave near Güzelyurt. The Byzantine duke of the time demanded taxes from the local population. Mamas refused to pay, since he lived in a cave as a hermit with no income. The Duke commanded two of his soldiers to arrest Mamas and bring him to Lefkoşa. As the soldiers brought Mamas to the city to be punished, they crossed paths with an aggressive lion about to pounce on a lamb and tear it apart. Mamas, witnessed by the terrified soldiers, saved the lamb from the lion's paws and continued the rest of the journey into the city on the back of the lion, carrying the lamb in his arms. On seeing, the Byzantine authorities were so impressed that they decided to exempt him from paying taxes for the rest of his life. Since then, Agios Mamas has been the patron saint of tax avoiders, a popular sport in Greece.

**Archaeology Museum** (open daily 09.00-18.30 in summer, 09.00-16.30 in winter), located in what was the bishop's residence. Next door is the curiously named **Agias Mamas Church**, which at some time changed gender. A relief on the wall outside shows the male saint, *Agios* Mamas riding his lion, but the church is now known as *Agias* (the Greek word for a female saint). There are no saints in the Muslim religion to provide an explanation. The tomb of Agios Mamas (on the left as you enter by the north door), is surrounded by votive offerings, many in the shape of ears.

Continue by following signs to Lefke which take you round three sides of the museum, and you pass the eye-catching mosque before leaving town. More orange, lemon, apricot, plum and even grapefruit trees accompany you to Gemikonağı, where you turn left to Lefke.

Copper has been mined on these lower slopes of the Troodos Mountains for at least 5000 years, and **Lefke** prospered on mining right up until 1960. Now, at the roundabout as you enter the town, an orange monument shows exactly how Lefke now earns its wealth. There is a graffiti-covered railway engine at the side of the road as a reminder of its mining past. Slag heaps, spoil heaps and copper-blue reservoirs above the town indicate the former scale of the operations. Lefke has been a Muslim Cypriot stronghold ever since the Ottoman invasion and possibly before. The town itself is a museum of Ottoman architecture, sadly much of it crumbling, but worth leaving the car to wander around. Men in turbans are not an unusual sight: they are followers of Shaikh Nazim, leader of the Naqshbandi-Haggani Sufi Order, who spends much of the year in Lefke. This order is a Muslim sect dedicated to bringing greater piety to North Cyprus (but without notable success).

Street scene in Lefke

Return to the coast road and continue past rusting iron jetties — another reminder of the decline in mining activities. After passing through **Gemikonağı**, watch for the sign on the left to **Soli** (open daily, 09.00-18.45 in summer, 09.00-16.45 in winter, small entry charge). The origins of this ancient site reach back to the 6th century BC; it was one of the ten city-kingdoms into which Cyprus was divided at the time. What remains today is mainly from the Roman period. The covered **basilica** is the first stopping point. This is one of the first churches built on Cyprus and is mainly from the 6th century AD. The canopy might add nothing to the atmosphere, but it does protect a floor covered with some wonderful mosaics, especially the swan. Further up the hillside is a **theatre** which has been so overly restored that the ancient atmosphere is now lost. The **agora** lies to the west of the pay booth, but there is little standing above ground level.

Continuing along the coast road towards Vouni, notice the fish restaurants on the sea side in **Yedidalga**, particularly Aspava and King Fish next door (see opposite).

Then watch for the Vouni sign on the right and follow the winding road to the top of the hill. Located at 230m (755ft), **Vouni Palace** certainly offered a room with a view — probably many rooms with extensive views. There is a small charge to enter, if the man collecting the fee is not soundly asleep (open daily 10.00-17.00 in summer, 09.00-13.00 and 14.00-16.45 in winter). Its origins are not known with certainty, but the palace is thought to have been built during the Persian occupation in the 5th century BC. There was constant warring with pro-Athenian Soli nearby. The palace was burnt down in 330 BC and abandoned around 400 BC. Little of its history is known — not even its original name (*vouni* just means 'mountain' in Greek). There is plenty to see, and the various rooms are well marked.

Return to Kyrenia by the outward route.

# Aspava and King Fish

You can have a good lunch at either of these seaside restaurants. **Aspava** sits above the narrow shingle shore with views out over the water. There are changing cubicles and a wooden pier with picnic tables. Popular with the locals. **King Fish** is next door to Aspava, but smaller; it also fronts the narrow shingle beach

Aspava (above right); *mineri* at Aspava (below); King Fish (bottom)

**ASPAVA**
**coast road, Yedidalga ☎ (0392) 7277621**
**daily (verify out of season) ££-£££**

**mezes** can include octopus or squid in vinegar

**fresh fish** like *mineri* (illustrated), swordfish, *sipya* (cuttlefish)

***lahmacun*, kebabs**

home-made **desserts**

wide range of **omelettes**

**KING FISH**
**coast road, Yedidalga ☎ (0392) 7277350 or (0533) 8664387**
**daily, but check out of season ££**

**fresh fish** of the day

***kup kebap*, *şiş* kebaps, meze** plate

1

Farming is the main occupation of the Koruçam villagers, and this fairly level walk meanders through the surrounding fields where, in springtime, flowers and orchids flourish. There is also the added possibility of bird life on the reservoir after a wet winter.

## koruçam circuit

# WALK

**Distance:** 9km/5.6mi; 2h50min

**Grade:** easy-moderate track walk, with one moderate downhill/uphill section — or opt for the 'Level' route below. After heavy winter rain, the track and valley bottom can be very muddy in places.

**Equipment:** see page 22

**Transport:** 🚗 car or taxi to Koruçam (see map on pages 28-29

**Refreshments:** Yorgos Kasap, opposite Koruçam church, or Golya Café/Restaurant at Sadrazamköy

**Level walk option** (2h40min). At the 40min-point fork right on a minor track, with excellent views towards Koruçam over to the right and mainly pine woods over to the left. In January, the track may be ploughed for a short distance — if so, keep more or less ahead to relocate the track (do not stray too far from the pine woods over to the left). Soon the track is close to the edge of the valley on the left, and you rejoin the main route, picking up the notes at the 1h30min point (where a track joins, rising up from the valley on the left).

Nestling in the foothills, at the extreme western edge of the Kyrenia Mountains, Koruçam is the centre of a Christian Maronite community, which has many similarities to the Greek Orthodox church. The Maronites originated in Syria in the seventh century, from where they moved to Lebanon to escape persecution, then over to Cyprus around the twelfth century. Many in this multi-lingual community use Greek as their main language, but also speak Turkish, English and a form of Arabic known as 'Sanna'. The huge church of St George dominates the village centre and is pivotal to Sunday worship.

**Start the walk** from the **church**, with your back to the main entrance. Go left, then immediately right, between houses No 1 and No 2. Stay ahead, ignoring roads off right and left, to wind through the village in a southerly direction. Meet the main road and cross over. Continue ahead on tarmac and

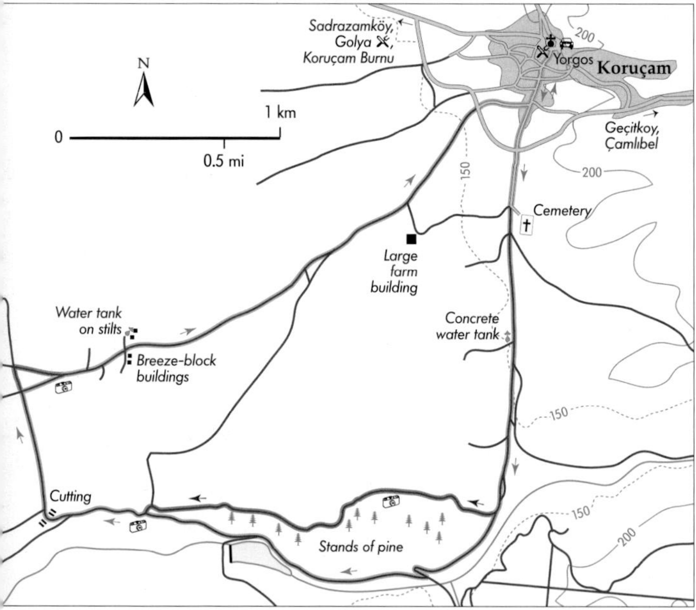


stay ahead as the road goes left (**12min**) towards the **cemetery**. Now on a track, ignore other tracks right and left. Pass a **concrete water tank** on the right and, 120m further on, keep right at a distinct fork (**30min**). After another 500m, the track divides, but soon rebraids itself (**40min**). Just after this stay ahead *(but take the right fork for the level option).*

Before long you begin a gradual descent which becomes steeper as the track makes a U-bend to the left, to the valley bottom. Turn sharp right here along the valley floor, with a stream bed on the left. Enjoy level walking for a while now, before the track begins a gentle ascent towards the **reservoir**. Just before reaching the **dam wall**, fork right uphill to a track junction (**1h30min**) at the top. *(The level walk option rejoins here from the right.)*

Birdwatchers on the approach to the reservoir

Turn left to continue. Ignore a track off left at the bottom of a dip in the track, after which the track then rises and bends sharply right to pass through a small cutting. Stay ahead as a track joins from the left. Koruçam, with its dominant church, is soon spotted through the trees to the right. Just under 600m past the cutting (around 10min; **1h50min**), watch carefully for a minor crossing track and turn right, straight towards Koruçam church. (If you miss this turn, turn right on a stronger crossing track 140m further on.) Soon, when you join a stronger track, turn right. This track winds between a group of **breeze block farm buildings** and a **water tank on stilts**. After passing a **large farm building** off to the right, you reach the main road. Cross it and continue ahead, to rejoin the outward route at a T-junction. Turn left, back to the square and church in **Koruçam** (**2h50min**).

# Yorgo Restaurant

This home-spun but renowned meat restaurant in the heart of Koruçam is very popular at weekends, especially on Sundays, when Greeks visit the church opposite, and *kleftiko* is the speciality of the day. The meat, yoghurt and cheese are all locally sourced and excellent. If you're only after a light lunch, just stay with *mezes* — or make sure you specify a *small* portion of meat! The meat is sold by weight; half a kilo is plenty for two normal appetites.

**YORGO RESTAURANT**
**Koruçam centre**
**( ask for Maria on (0533) 8642772 or 392 7242060**
**daily ex Mon, all year, for lunch and dinner ££**

**locally sourced meat** — lamb chops, kebabs, chicken and the like, accompanied by a selection of **meze** dishes

**local cheese** and **yoghurt**

***kleftiko*** is the **Sunday speciality**

home-made **red wine**, served in a 1.5 litre water bottle, is good but expensive

Yorgo's (below) and their *kleftiko* ovens (right)

restaurants

eat

## Golya Restaurant

**GOLYA RESTAURANT**
**Sadrazamköy**
**☎ (0533) 8603934**
**all year, Sun-Thu 11.00-20.00, Fri-Sat 11.00-midnight; cl Tue ££**

**good menu** for its isolated location

**fish of the day**, **chops** or **steak** with **salad**

***kleftiko*** cooked in a clay oven on Sundays; ***manti***

**kebabs**, ***makarna tavuk***

**lighter fare**: sandwiches, salads, selection of 5 *mezes*

The last outpost before the tip of Cape Koruçam (Kormakíti), the hamlet of Sadrazamköy is the nearest point on North Cyprus to the Turkish mainland, just 74km away. Golya's is even further along the cape, where the tarmac ends at a new development. (The stabilised track to the cape beyond the restaurant is fine for cars.) Golya's gets its name from a farm, now a ruin, located between Koruçam and Sadrazamköy. It is Turkish Cypriot owned. Everything is cooked to order, so service can be a bit slow if they're busy — but it's easy to sit in the sun and enjoy a drink while you wait. If you want Sunday *kleftiko* here, it's best to telephone the previous Friday to order.

Golya (left) and their *manti*

# KLEFTIKO

Traditionally *kleftiko* (Greek; called *kup kebap* or *hirsiz kebap* in Turkish — 'thieves kebap') is cooked very slowly in a clay oven, either individually or in large tins with potato wedges. To make it yourself, choose shanks from lamb or goat (the latter are more highly regarded in North Cyprus). Tell the butcher you want meat for *kleftiko*. If a shank is large it will serve two people.

For the individual method, wrap each shank in a large parcel of foil, with a sprinkle of salt, oregano & bay leaf; slices of carrot and onion could also be added. Seal and place in a clay dish or roasting tin. For the tray method, arrange the shanks in a large casserole dish or a metal cooking tray, interspersed with potato wedges. Use ample seasoning as above; seal with foil. Cook the parcels for about 3h, the large trays 4h — both at 160° C.

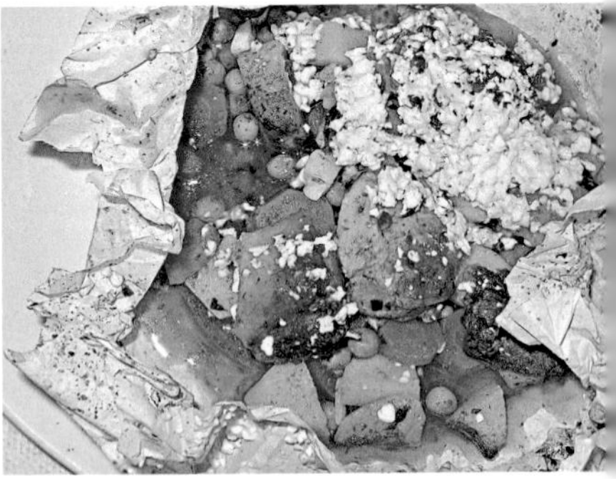

But you can make this tasty approximation of *kleftiko* that cooks much more quickly (see method opposite).

Ingredients (for 2 people)

300 g lean lamb, cubed
2 tbsp olive oil
1 small onion, finely chopped
1 garlic clove, pressed
1 potato, cut into small cubes
1 carrot, thinly sliced
60 g frozen peas
2 tbsp lemon juice
1/2 tsp dried oregano
salt & black pepper
1 medium tomato, sliced & cored
50 g *beyaz peynir* or Lancashire cheese, crumbled or cubed
2 large squares of tin foil, greased

## Quick lamb *kleftiko*

Preheat the oven to 180° C. Brown the meat cubes in 1 tbsp of the olive oil. Add a further 1 tbsp of olive oil and soften the onion, carrot and potato, stirring.

After a couple of minutes add the garlic, peas, oregano, salt & pepper. Cook a further couple of minutes.

Divide the mixture evenly and place in the middle of the foil sheets. Gather up the sides of the foil a little to form a bowl. Scatter over the cheese, place tomato slices on the top and sprinkle a little more oregano over. Gather the sides of the foil in, to form a sealed parcel and place in a roasting tin. Cook in the oven on 180 °C about an hour, then serve immediately.

## *Manti* (Turkish pasta with yoghurt & pepper sauce, *illustrated on page 49*)

*Manti* originated in Central Asia as a meat filled-pasta (*Tartar böreği*, 'borek of the Tartars'). The dried version is more commonly used.

Cook the *manti* in boiling water for about 20min. Meanwhile, grate the *helim* and mix with some dried mint. Cover a plate with this mix. Mix the onion and garlic into the yoghurt.

For the sauce, melt the butter in a pan and add the red pepper powder and olive oil. Mix well. (Or just use your favourite spicy, sweet/sour sauce – there is plenty of scope for experiment!)

Ingredients (for 1 person)

40 g *helim* cheese (approx)
150 g *manti* pasta
dried mint to taste
200 g yoghurt
1 garlic clove, crushed
1 small onion, grated

*For the sauce*

1 tsp red pepper powder
20 g butter
olive oil to taste

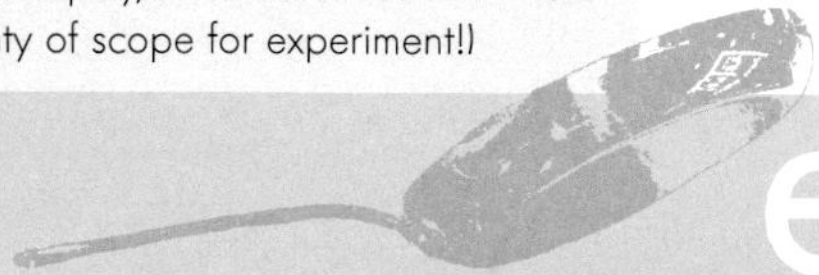

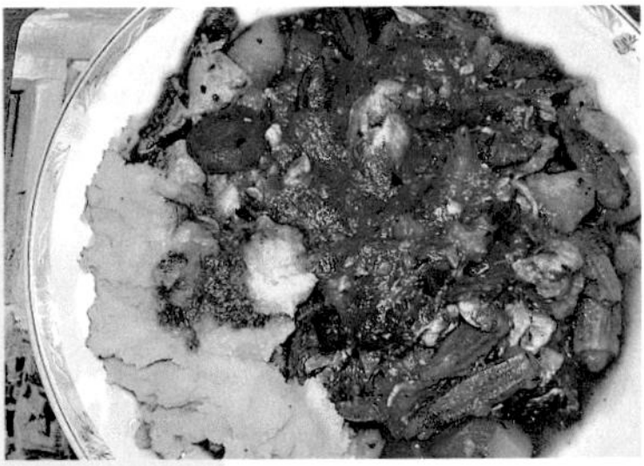

## *Etli turlu* (Meat stew)

Soften the onions in the oil, then brown the meat quickly. Add all the vegetables except the peas and tomatoes. Turn the contents of the pan to coat with the pan juices and add salt (if needed), pepper and herbs. Sauté gently.

After a few minutes, pour over the water or stock; lower the heat and leave to cook gently for about 45min. Add peas and tomatoes and, if needed, a little more water. Continue to cook until tender. Adjust the seasoning and serve with rice or bulgar with vermicelli

Ingredients (for 4 people)

- 750 g lamb, veal, lean beef; ask for it to be cut 'şiş' (cubed), or chicken
- 2 large onions, sliced, or 10 shallots
- 2 carrots, sliced
- 2 potatoes, peeled & cubed
- 2 courgettes, sliced
- 2 tomatoes, chopped
- a handful of peas (optional)
- a few okra (*bamya*); clean & cut the tops into a cone shape, to retain the seeds
- 1/2 tsp of mixed dried herbs
- 2 tbsp olive oil
- 220 ml water or stock (made with 1 chicken, veg or beef stock cube)
- salt & black pepper

## *Siyah zeytin ezmesi* (Black olive paste; *not illustrated*)

Blend together 150 g fat black oily olives, 2 crushed garlic cloves and 50 ml olive oil until fairly smooth. Store in the fridge with a shallow covering of olive oil and serve as a starter with bread. Keeps for weeks and will also freeze.

Around the end of March into April bundles of fresh wild asparagus appear for sale in supermarkets, wayside stalls and from anyone who takes the trouble to search it out. More straggly than the plumper versions grown commercially, it is exquisite when fresh. The easy recipe below was shown us by a Greek friend from Lesvos. We both went out with him to collect asparagus then, back at his home, he said the best way for Eileen to learn was to prepare the asparagus and make the omelette herself!

No quantity is given for the asparagus, as the egg is used just to bind a panful. Use your judgement to increase the quantity of asparagus, and add an extra two eggs to the recipe per extra person.

We have had a similar concoction, made for us in Turkey, using fresh young french beans in place of asparagus.

## *Ayrelli omlet* (Wild asparagus omelette; *not illustrated*)

Prepare the asparagus by snapping off pieces, starting at the tip, until the stem resists snapping. Discard the woody bottom piece. Place all the pieces in a pan of boiling water for 5min, to remove bitterness, then drain.

Beat the eggs and add seasoning and milk. In a frying pan, soften the onion, then add the drained asparagus pieces and sauté a few minutes.

Pour the egg over and mix with the asparagus and onion. Cook gently until the egg is just set and serve immediately.

Ingredients (for 2 people)

- 4 eggs (beaten)
- 1 bunch wild asparagus or 250 g approximately
- 1 medium onion, finely chopped (more if desired)
- 2 tbsp olive oil or butter
- 2 tbsp milk or cream
- salt & black pepper

This rewarding walk visits a hidden oasis within the folds of the Kyrenia mountain range which abounds with wild flowers in springtime and where the black tulip (*Tulipa cypria*) has a foothold. Sightings of birds are also a bonus after a wet winter, but the distinctive call of the black francolin is often heard.

# geçitköy reservoir circuit

# WALK 2

**Distance:** 8km/5mi; 2h40min

**Grade:** moderate, along tracks, with an overall height gain of 125m/410ft

**Equipment:** see page 22

**Transport:** 🚗 to Geçitköy (see map on pages 28-29). Around 0.6km from the mosque in Geçitköy, as the road ascends and bends to the right, turn left on a rough, stabilised track. This leads to the right-hand top of the dam; park at the side.

**Refreshments:** Hasan's Café/Restaurant in Geçitköy; Aphrodite and others along the coast road on the return

**Alternative** (5km/3mi). Use the map to walk along the return route for the circuit, going as far as the feeder stream for the reservoir and returning the same way. This is an easier option, greener, and has the most floristic interest.

**Start out** by crossing the **dam wall**. The track rises and dips along the contours above the reservoir below on your right, offering differing perspectives inland. Just after the track descends in a U-bend to the left, note a path off right. This is a good short-cut any time, but especially after heavy rain if the track is muddy. But it *does* require a short scramble to regain the track at the far side.

If you stay on the track and round the bend, you will rise to pass a track (**20min**) joining sharply from above you to the left. Stay along the main track here, heading in the same general direction along the hillside and ignoring tracks right and left.

You cross a **fire-break** after 2km and 1.5km further on, after descending gradually, you reach a **ruined breeze block building** and then a **disused fountain** on the left. This makes a pleasant picnic spot, either in the open or under the trees on the right. At a **track junction** almost immediately (**1h24min**), turn right downhill, descending steadily to the valley bottom. Ignore

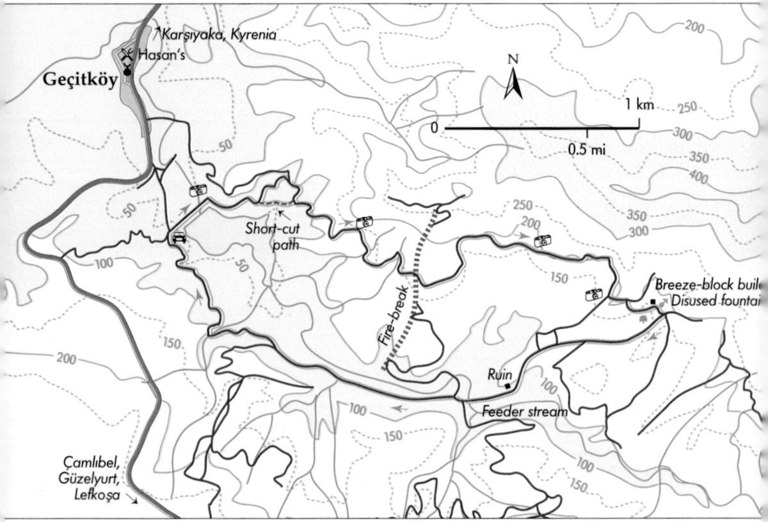


a track joining sharply from the right and, a few minutes later, pass a **ruin** on the right as the track bends right. The route becomes more rural as the track dips to cross the **feeder stream to the reservoir (1h50min)**. Stay ahead to return, through the most floristic section of the walk in spring, back to the **dam wall (2h40min)** — again, ignoring tracks left and right.

Mountain views during the early part of the walk

# Avcılar Restaurant (Hasan's)

You'll find Hasan's restaurant near the mosque in Geçitköy; look for the clay oven in front. Hasan is quite a character and loves to chat (he had a kebab restaurant in London before returning to Cyprus because he missed his goats). He butchers all his own meat, keeps the place spotless and does the cooking; his wife makes the yoghurt and cheese. The café next door is run by his cousin (who rustled up a really good freshly made *ayran* for us).

Eat at Hasan's for a truly local experience. The menu is simple, but varied; all food is home-made from local produce and delicious. Although there is not much for vegetarians, Hasan would probably produce some pasta. It is amazing what willing people like Hasan can conjure up to satisfy their customers. The clay oven is lit on weekends for the *küp kebap* speciality. It may not be necessary to order one in advance, but it is advisable.

Hasan in front of his restaurant, with his clay oven

**AVCILAR (HASAN'S)**
**Geçitköy centre ☎ (0533) 8798870**
**daily, all year, from breakfast; cl Mon £**

**lamb**, **chicken** and some **goat** in various guises, cooked on the grill

***küp kebap*** is the weekend **speciality**

**eggs**, **omelettes**, **salads** for a lighter meal

***doner kebaps*** (a good lunch time snack), **chicken *şiş***, **wings**, and **breast** with ***helim* cheese**; ***adana kebap***, ***şeftali***

main courses served with **salad**, **cacık**, ***turşu***, local **bread** and fresh **fruit** or a Cypriot **dessert**

# Aphrodite Restaurant

Aphrodite is an unexpected experience. To find it, head back along the coast road from Lapta towards Girne. Pass 'Flippers Bungalows' on the right and the left turn to the Sempati Hotel, then turn left on the next narrow road (by Sevket's Restaurant). Aphrodite is at the end, on the right, near the coast — a modern building but with an older ambience. If no-one is around, ring Cemal (the owner) in the first instance. He'll probably come roaring up in his truck.

Cemal and his guests enjoy some post-prandial dancing.

Cemal is a larger-than-life character in combat outfit and beret. It comes as no surprise that he is a great fan of 'Monty' (Viscount Montgomery) and speaks English as well as Greek. Even a horse or donkey might put in an appearance.

Cemal makes his own wine and is happy for you to taste before deciding on white or red. Or try the home-made lemonade. For a treat to finish, try the pancakes or the Cypriot preserve *macun* with coffee.

**APHRODITE RESTAURANT**
**on the coast at Lapta**
**☎ Cemal (0542) 8538792, Cemile (0533) 8636231 or Keziban (0533) 8606970**
**daily, all year, from lunchtime** ££

**traditional Cypriot food** – *stifado, mousaka,* lamb chops, chicken, *köfte*

**locally sourced** meat, cheese, yoghurt; home-grown vegetables

**mezes** (including seasonal dishes like caper leaves in vinegar or artichokes with egg), *cacık, nor* (a soft cheese)

**fresh fish** & 1 **vegetarian** dish

restaurants

eat

## *Kibrisli kolokas* (*Kolokas* with chicken)

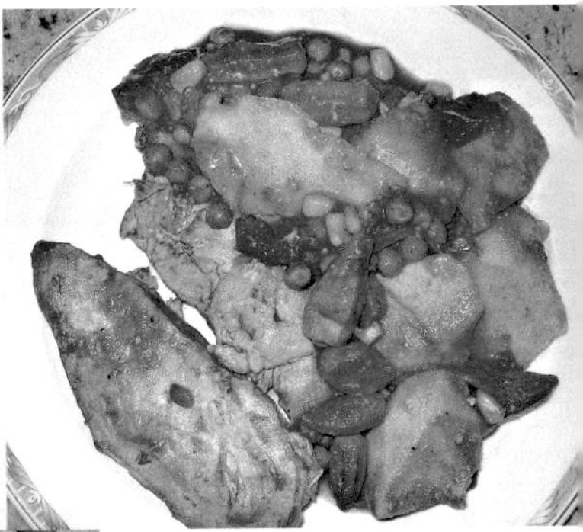

*Kolokas* is an unusual root vegetable, which looks rather like a sweet potato. It's readily available and very tasty when used in stews. This is a quick and easy recipe.

Fry the chicken in oil to brown on both sides. Remove, set aside, and fry the onion to soften.

*Kolokas* on sale in the market

Ingredients (for 2 people)

- 500 g chicken (breasts or joints)
- 500 g *kolokas*
- oil for frying (2 tbsp vegetable + tbsp olive oil)
- 1 small onion, finely chopped
- 2 sticks celery, thickly sliced
- 1/2 tbsp tomato paste (mix with stock) or 1 tin of chopped tomatoes (in which case, reduce the stock to 200 ml)
- 500 ml chicken stock, heated
- salt & pepper

Peel the *kolokas*, break off bite-size chunks, and place in a heavy-bottomed pan. Add all the other ingredients, including the fried chicken and onion.

Bring to the boil, then cover and cook over a low heat, stirring occasionally, for about 30min.

Sweeping panoramic views and sleepy mountain villages feature in this excursion along the foothills of the Kyrenia Mountains – a delight at any time except high summer. İlgaz was once a Greek village and the abandoned church is still the dominant landmark for the walk's ultimate destination.

# alsancak and ilgaz

# WALK 3

Start the walk from **Alsancak post office** by briefly continuing west towards Lapta. Take the first left turn (Gençlik Sokak; signposted to Incesu and Malatya). Follow this road inland, ignoring roads off left and right. After passing Minik Sokak off right (**12min**), you'll notice a dry river valley on the right. The river bed becomes more apparent as the village is left behind. As the road bends right in a U, **The Old Mill** is ahead (**20min**). Wide steps on the left are the return route.

Follow the track to the left of The Old Mill, with the ruins of the original mill over to the right. After a short stiff climb, ignore a track joining from the left. Stay ahead round a U-bend and soon rise out of the valley, where the incline lessens. The track is now running alongside a deep valley on the left. Ignore a

**Distance:** 11km/6.9mi; 3h40min

**Grade:** moderate; along tracks with an overall height gain of 200m/660ft

**Equipment:** see page 22

**Transport:** 🚐 to the centre of Alsancak; alight at the post office. Regular service from Girne. Some Lapta buses also go through Alsancak; ask the driver. Or 🚗: see options below for alternative starting points.

**Refreshments:** 2 fast food places and Cenap in Alsancak centre; Tervetuloa in Alsancak; Hoots in İlgaz; The Black Olive Café at Incesu; Green Heights north of İlgaz

**Shorter option 1:** 8.7km/5.4mi; 3h. 🚗 Drive the route of the walk to the 20min-point — the Old Mill Restaurant in Alsancak (now defunct), and park there. This is a one-way system, so when driving away continue round the bend and follow the arrows in the village back to the main road. Turn right back to the centre.

**Shorter option 2:** 4.8km/3mi; 1h40min. 🚗 to Malatya; park at the entrance to the village, where the road bends right and Malatya Café/Bar is on the right-hand corner. Start the walk here by continuing along the road through the village. Around 5 minutes later, pick up the main walk at the 1h20min-point.

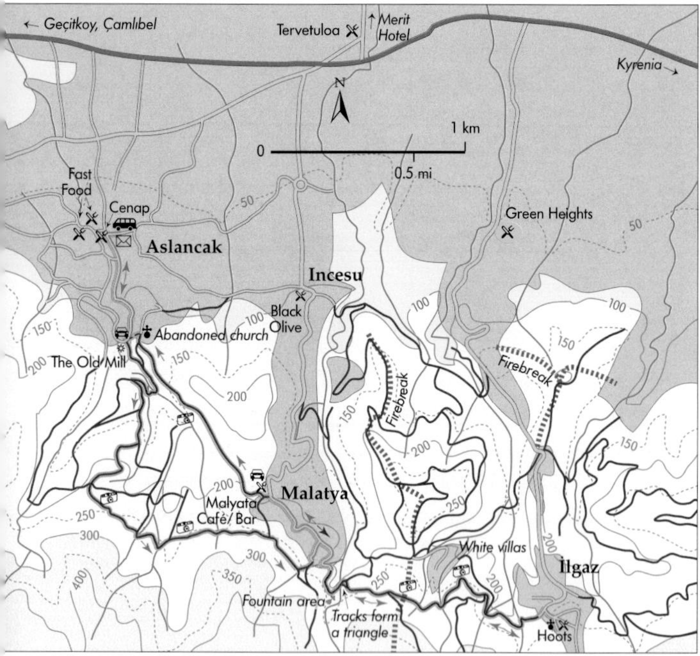


minor track joining from the right and two tracks heading left downhill into the valley (**40min**). There are valleys left and right now, before you rise to a crossing track. Go straight over and follow this high level track past any minor offshoots, to continue uphill. Enjoy good views and a level section at the top of the rise, before dipping to wind round the heads of two valleys.

Reach the top of the next rise (just over **1h**) and start to descend towards Malatya. At a T-junction, go right uphill to skirt behind the village. On approaching a gully at the edge of the village, turn left downhill on a stony track. Meet a track and continue left downhill. After the track bends left and becomes tarmac, go right downhill to the main village street in **Malatya** (**1h20min**). Turn right. *(Option 2 joins here.)*

Soon start into a deep U-bend, where the road reverts to track. A shaded **fountain area** at the head of the gorge provides a good rest spot, but the once-spectacular waterfall has dried up due to lack of rain and a lowering of the water table. Ascend again to a track junction and take the second of the two tracks to the right (the two tracks form a triangle and rejoin, but the second track is easier). At the next junction stay ahead (left); do not go uphill to the right. Again, at a further junction, *ignore* the right fork, uphill, and stay ahead, to start to descend. You will notice a cluster of **white villas** over to the left. The track swings right alongside another valley, and İlgaz comes into view on the far side. Descend to round the valley bottom and rise to meet a track, where you keep right, uphill. The abandoned Greek church in the village is clearly visible. On coming into **İlgaz**, turn right (there is a signpost to Hoots restaurant). At crossroads, turn right to pass the Greek **church** on the right, **car park** and **ruined school**. Hoots (**2h**) is on the left.

To retrace your route back to Malatya for the return, walk back through İlgaz and turn left downhill. After turning left again to skirt round the valley bottom, retrace the track back towards Malatya, ignoring joining tracks. When you come to the point where the two tracks form a triangle, turn left on the crossing track just beyond them and head into **Malatya**. Stay ahead through the village and, where the road sweeps right downhill *(at the start of Option 2)*, keep ahead on a track. Malatya Café/Bar is on the right (and another café, The Black Olive, is lower downhill to the right, along the road at Incesu).

Start into the descent to Alsancak on what was once the old cobbled route between the villages and to the mill. This is a pleasant descent with wide-ranging views. On reaching habitation, follow the track to the right as another joins from the left. A forlorn **Greek church** sits amongst the olive trees on the right. Just before the track becomes tarmac, go down the path to the left (opposite the church gates). The descending path bends right and left, passes the front of a house, and goes down wide stone steps, back to the road by the **Old Mill**. Turn right, back to **Alsancak** centre (**3h40min**).

If you're looking for a light meal in the centre, try either the **Dolphin Café** (£) or the **Fast Food Café** (£); they are almost opposite each other in the centre, near the post office. Both serve excellent snacks and simple meals. Fast Food Café is very popular for its *doner kebaps* (wraps).

A groaning spread of *mezes* at Cenap (top) and relaxing at Hoots (right)

# Hoots Bar & Restaurant

*(photograph opposite, below)*

A special place secreted in the village of İlgaz, cosy in winter and delightful in the secluded courtyard or on the roof terrace in summer. Run by Sonia and Murat ('Kevin'), it is a lovely relaxing place, even if you just drop in for a drink.

**HOOTS BAR & RESTAURANT**
**ilgaz ( (0542) 8738068/8747305**
**daily, all year, ex Mon 11.00-21.30; order evening meals in advance** ££
**home-cooked English** and **Cypriot** dishes
**light lunches, snacks**

A very tasty and light lunch is the house *helim* salad (see page 68). The lunch selection, which can be just a sandwich, varies, as do the evening meals, but all the food is delicious. When arranged in advance, Sonia can rustle up a great *meze*-style buffet for a special occasion or group. Whatever, it is a lovely relaxing place if only to drop in for a drink.

# Cenap Restaurant

*(photograph opposite, top)*

**CENAP RESTAURANT**
**Alsancak centre ( (0392) 8218417/ 8213020**
**all year, cl Mon; only in the evening; booking advised £££**
vast array of **meze** dishes
one of the best **kebab** houses in North Cyprus

Its location in the middle of Alsancak may not look promising, but go inside (although there is outside dining in summer). Never-ending *mezes* and meat dishes — a meal here is one to linger over and enjoy in the company of a few friends with healthy appetites. Fixed prices are excellent value.

# Tervetuloa Hotel & Restaurant

A favourite venue of Northern Cypriots and visitors, owned and run by a Cypriot family. As usual, mum does the cooking, dad tends the bar, and daughter oversees the restaurant. A pleasant dining room is abandoned in summer for the large courtyard, partially shaded by a huge foxglove tree.

**TERVETULOA**
**near Alsancak ( (0392) 8211220/ 8211229; or mob (0542) 8514140; in high season, book a table!**
**daily, all year, lunch and dinner ££**

extensive **menu**, including **Cypriot specialities** like *kleftiko*, *molohiya*, fish in a roof tile, chicken with onions, etc

**complimentary** *meze* starters, coffee and brandy

To find Tervetuloa from Alsancak, head along the main coast road towards Kyrenia. Soon (just past the 'Golden Lady' statue on the inland side of the road), turn left, seawards, towards the Merit Hotel. Tervetuloa is on the left, where a narrow road joins from the left *before* the Merit Hotel. Turn left up the narrow road to park behind the restaurant.

An amazing and complimentary array of *meze* starters happily fill in time before the main course arrives (a wide range of drinks is available). After … a small baklava, fruit, coffee and brandy to finish.

# Green Heights

A classic setting in an unexpected location, this delightful green oasis never fails to amaze. Wander the grounds, lounge on a hammock, or just sit and absorb the soporific atmosphere — drink in hand. A magnet is the magnificent swimming pool which mirrors the white tent-like restaurant.

**GREEN HEIGHTS**
**Green Heights Botanic Gardens**
**( (0533) 8627656; daily all year, from breakfast to dinner ££**

English or Cypriot **breakfast**

**light meals:** sandwiches, burgers (try a mango burger!), omelettes, salads (like the smoked salmon shown on page 9 or caesar *(sezar)*, soups, pastas

**grills** — chicken, pork, lamb, salmon

excellent **Cypriot desserts**

large **drinks** selection (including pomegranate juice in season)

To get there, turn inland off the main coast road west (coming from Kyrenia), sign-posted to Yeşiltepe and İlgaz, shortly after passing the Illeli and Starling Supermarkets on the left. The Green Heights Botanic Gardens are about 1km along, on the left. Admission to the garden is free, but there is a charge to use the swimming pool, which is reduced if buying a meal (not just a snack).

## *Helim* & aubergine salad

Griddle or grill the aubergines, drizzled with a touch of olive oil, tomatoes and *helim*. When softened, layer in a stack on 4 plates; a slice of tomato first, then *helim*, then aubergine — with pieces of rocket in between, until there are 4 layers on each plate. Pour over some balsamic vinegar and garnish with the remaining rocket.

Ingredients (for 4 people)

- 3-4 aubergines (enough for 16 x 1-cm thick slices; the smaller end pieces can be added)
- 4 large tomatoes, sliced (more if smaller)
- 16 slices of *helim* cheese
- 1 bunch of rocket (*roka*)
- balsamic vinegar
- little olive oil to drizzle sparsely over the aubergines

## *Keşkül* (Almond milk pudding; *not illustrated*)

As easy to make as custard. Beat the egg yolks, then whisk with the sugar, almond essence, cornflour, and milk. Pour into a pan and stir over a medium heat. Add the ground almonds when the surface bubbles and boil for 1 min, stirring. Cool a little before pouring into individual bowls and put in the fridge to chill. Garnish with some ground pistachio.

Ingredients (for 6 people)

- 1 litre of full cream milk
- 4 egg yolks
- 1 tsp almond essence
- 30 g (2 tbsp) cornflour (*nişasta*)
- 100 g sugar
- 75 g ground almonds

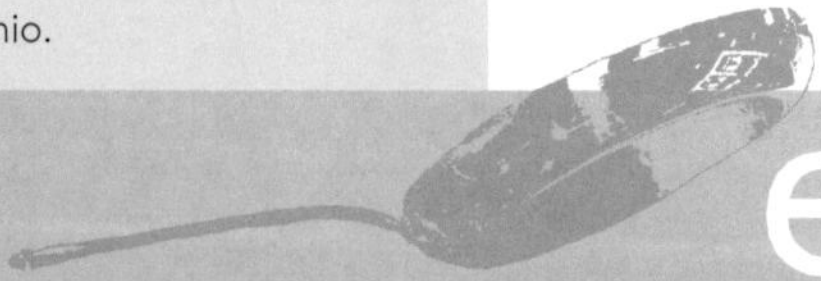

recipes

eat

## *Kuru fasulye* (Bean casserole)

Sonia at Hoots makes a particularly tasty version of this dish.

Cover the dried beans with water to 4-5cm (1 inch) above the beans and leave overnight to soak. Drain and rinse the beans. Put in a pan of fresh water and boil for 10min, then reduce the heat and simmer for a further 45min-1h, or until just cooked (the beans still need to be fairly firm). Drain and rinse the beans in warm water.

In a pan or flame-proof casserole dish, soften the onions and brown the cubed meat (if used). Add garlic, chopped tomato, tomato paste, cumin (or other spice), black pepper and stock cube dissolved in the water. Bring to the boil and simmer about 20min to make a sauce.

Add the beans and continue to simmer – uncovered to thicken the sauce if necessary, for a further 20-30min, until the beans are soft. Add the parsley/dill and optional spicy sausage around 10min before cooking time ends.

To serve more like a soup, cover the pan to retain moisture. Check seasoning; it may need more cumin and salt & pepper. Add more water if required.

Ingredients (for 4 people)

- 200 g dried haricot/cannellini beans
- 2 onions, chopped
- 2 garlic cloves, crushed, or 2 tsp minced garlic
- 2 tomatoes, skinned & chopped
- 1 tbsp tomato paste
- 1 chicken stock cube
- 1 *carliston* pepper (sweet) or a red pepper, chopped
- 2 tsp cumin (or try 1/4 tsp chilli flakes or 1/2 tsp cayenne or even 1/4 tsp *acı biber*)
- 1/2 bunch fresh parsley or dill, chopped
- salt (to taste) & black pepper
- 600 ml water
- small cubes of lamb (optional)
- slices of spicy sausage (*sucuk*, optional)

Molohiya chicken

## *Molohiya*

Similar to spinach, but with a more herbaceous flavour, *molohiya* is an acquired taste for non-Cypriot palates. But a good *molohiya* dish, made with lamb or chicken, can be delicious. Look in the vegetable section in supermarkets for bags of dried *molohiya,* but fresh is sometimes available (which needs less cooking).

Ingredients (for 4 people)

- 160 g dried molohiya or 500 g fresh
- 500 g lamb or chicken, cut into bite size pieces
- 2 medium onions, chopped
- 4 garlic cloves, crushed
- 2 large tomatoes, skinned & chopped
- 1 tbsp tomato paste
- 1 lemon, juice of
- 90 ml (6 tbsp) sunflower or olive oil
- 800 ml chicken stock (2 stock cubes)
- 100 ml vinegar
- salt & black pepper

Soak dried *molohiya* overnight, then rinse thoroughly, drain well and squeeze out excess water. (Wash fresh *molohiya* and discard stalks and wilted leaves. Boil for 2min, drain then add to the meat.)

Heat the oil in a large pan and fry the lamb or chicken for a few minutes to seal, then remove from pan. Fry the onions to soften, then add the garlic. Return the chicken to the pan with the chopped tomatoes, tomato paste, salt, hot chicken stock, vinegar & black pepper. (Some cooks add a pinch of sugar at this stage.)

Now add the prepared *molohiya* and lemon juice and bring to the boil. Cover and simmer for 1h to 1h30min. (Fresh *molohiya* will take about 1h — or only 20min in a pressure cooker.)

## Balık güveç (Fish in a roof tile)

Preheat the oven to 180° C. Heat oil in a pan and soften the onions. Add the tomatoes, parsley, vinegar, salt & pepper and simmer to make a sauce. Gently mix the fish with the sauce and put into 2 oiled earthenware pots or 1 casserole dish. Lay slices of tomato over the top and add extra seasoning if needed. Bake at 180C for about 20-30min until the fish is cooked. Serve with the lemon wedges.

The name comes from the güveç, an earthenware pot — or 'roof tile'.

## Fasulye (Green beans; *not illustrated*)

Soften the onion and garlic in the olive oil, add the tomato, salt & black pepper and beans. Just cover with water and boil gently to cook the beans and reduce the water (about 25min). Add a drop more water if necessary, but the finished dish should have no excess water.

*Fasulye*: Ingredients (for 2 people)

250g runner beans, sliced
100 ml chopped tomato or 1 large tomato, skinned & chopped
1 small onion, finely chopped
1 garlic clove, finely chopped
1 tbsp olive oil
salt & black pepper

*Balık güveç*: Ingredients (for 2 people)

400 g firm white fleshy fish, cut into large chunks
3 tbsp olive oil
1 medium onion, chopped
2 large or 4 medium tomatoes (skin & chop one of the large tomatoes or 2 medium, and slice the rest for topping)
1/2 bunch fresh parsley, chopped
salt & black pepper
50ml vinegar
1/2 lemon, cut into wedges

Green Heights is the place to sample local desserts. Cypriot desserts are very sweet, so we have reduced the sugar content appreciably; sweet-tooths can always add extra. Here are two examples; another, *sütlaç*, is on page 103.

## *Kazandibi* (Caramelised milk pudding)

Preheat the oven to 220° C. Grease the base of a baking tin 25 cm x 30 cm x 3 cm. Sprinkle over the 45 g of sugar for the base.

*Kazandibi* is an Istanbul speciality.

Ingredients (for 6 people)

1 litre milk
65 g rice flour
34 g cornflour *(nişasta)*
150 g sugar
2-1/2 tsp vanilla essence
5 g butter
cinnamon to sprinkle on top (optional)

*For the caramel base*

45 g sugar

Put the tin in the hot oven until the sugar turns a light caramel colour, then remove and reduce the oven temperature to 180° C.

Combine the rice flour, cornflour and milk. Cook over a low heat, stirring, until thickened (or microwave). Stir in the sugar until dissolved, then cook a further 1min, still stirring. Remove from heat and stir in the vanilla.

Pour over the caramel base in the tin and bake 15-20min. Then place the tin in cold water and leave for 10min.

Turn out of tin and dust with cinnamon (optional). Cut into 6 slices and fold in half lengthwise. Chill in the fridge. Serve with yoghurt, ice cream or *kaymak* (Turkish cream).

## *Ekmek kadayıfı*

*Ekmek kadayıfı* is on sale in see-through packages at supermarket dessert counters; it's used to make a popular sweet known by the same name – a kind of syrup-soaked bread. There are different recipes for the syrup; this is an easy, tasty version.

Place the dry *ekmek* in a greased roasting tin or heatproof dish, the two halves side-by-side. Leave some room for the *ekmek* to expand. Dampen the dry *ekmek* with enough warm water to moisten. (Dampen the top half less at this stage, to make it easier to place over the bottom half after adding the filling.)

Make the syrup by bringing all the ingredients to the boil, then simmering 15-20min. Then remove the cloves and cinnamon stick.

Pour a little syrup over the lower layer, then spread with cheese and carefully cover with the other half. (Dampen the top half with a little more water at this stage if needed.)

Cook over a low heat, gradually pouring over the syrup until it has all been absorbed. Check every so often that the *kadayıfı* is not sticking. Leave in the tin/dish to cool 15-20min, then turn out onto a serving dish.

Ingredients (for 6-8 people)

1 small *(kuçuk) ekmek kadayıfı*
500 g *nor* (Turkish soft cheese) or cottage cheese
warm water to moisten

*For the syrup*

500 ml water
1 orange (juice of)
1/2 lemon (juice of)
100 g sugar
2 cloves
1 cinnamon stick

4

Perched high in the shelter of the Kyrenia Mountains, the pristine, 'model' village of Karaman could sit just as comfortably today in a Dorset countryside setting. Behind its current tranquillity lies an industrious past when carob mills, now restored as houses, harnessed the water from the abundant mountain streams.

# karaman circuit WALK

**Distance:** 4.6km/2.9mi; 1h40min

**Grade:** easy-moderate; along tracks and village roads, with an overall height gain of 190m/625ft

**Equipment:** see page 22

**Transport:** 🚗 to Karaman (see map on pages 28-29); park in the car park in the church square.

**Refreshments**: The Halfway House, on the road between Karaman and Edremit; Levant Bistro and Bar in Karaman

After 1974 the once-Greek village of Karaman was laid waste and deserted, until the offer of low rentals, in exchange for restoration of the houses, saw a reversal in fortunes. Today, it would easily win awards as the best-kept village in North Cyprus, especially when vibrantly in bloom in spring and summer. Before starting the walk, locate the old mill pond and explore the upper village by climbing the steps out of the car park.

**The walk starts** in **Church Square** (Kilise Medani) in **Karaman**. Head west along the road towards İlgaz. The tarmac becomes concrete, and there are panoramic views to the coast. When the route continues ahead as track (**8min**), turn left on concrete, but as the road bends left uphill, keep straight on, then fork right along a minor track heading towards the mountains. This section is great for views and flower- and bird-buffs in the spring. After about 600m you reach a **well-head** (**20min**).

Return the same way to the 8min-point and turn left downhill. The track dips and heads towards some **skeletal concrete structures**. Before the track junction in the dip, you pass a large **arched, abandoned structure** on the right. Ahead continues to İlgaz, but turn right downhill on a wide stony track. A **lone dwelling** sits on the bend here, with more abandoned

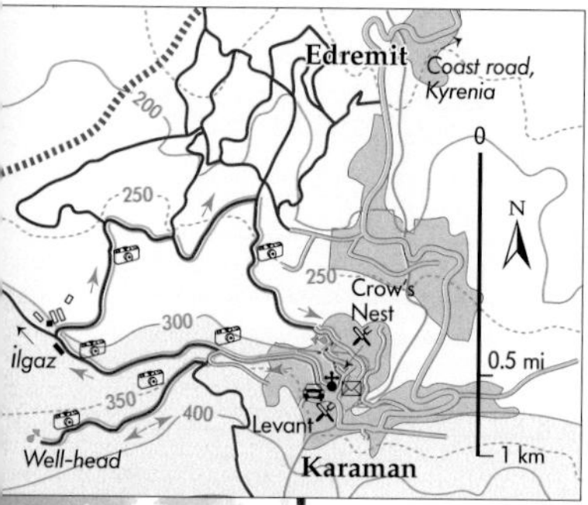


structures below. Now heading for the coast, ignore a track off left; stay on the descending track. This bends right and soon passes another track off left. Karaman eventually comes into view ahead, with the jagged peak of St Hilarion Castle behind it.

Returning from the well-head

At a T-junction, turn right uphill towards Karaman on a stabilised track. After a steepish climb, stay ahead below the village on **Cypress Road** (Selvi Sokak), to reach an **old fountain** on the right and **Poppysteps** (Gelincik Basamaklari). Turn right up these steps. At the top of the first flight (where more steps continue uphill to the right), stay ahead on the road. Ahead is another **fountain** and round *sarniç* (cistern). Reach more steps on the right, **Stony Walk** (Taşlik Geçigidi). Climb these cobbled steps and stay ahead on the road to a crossing road. Just downhill to the left is the Crow's Nest (bar/snacks). Turn right here towards an arched bridge over the road. On the left, before the bridge, is the **post office** and shop. Beyond the **bridge**, walk behind the **church** and then a seasonal **information office** on the left. Continue towards the **Levant Bistro** straight ahead, from where a right turn leads back to the **church square (1h40min)**.

# Levant Bistro

Two secluded, tree-shaded terraces at the rear of this bistro are a restful haven in summer. The upper terrace is a pleasant bar area, while diners on the lower terrace enjoy views along the mountainside to St Hilarion Castle. In winter a log fire creates a cosy ambience indoors. Although not strictly Cypriot, the food is very tasty and the location superb. At busy times book in advance!

**LEVANT BISTRO**
**Karaman centre, near the church square car park ✆ (0392) 8222559; daily 11.00-23.30, cl Mon & Feb ££-£££**

ideal for a **light lunch** of soup, chilli or various salads, all served with home-made bread

delicious selection on the main **menu** includes seasonal produce, like a starter of fresh artichoke with a lemon butter dip, followed by asparagus on a parmesan risotto or lamb

**sweets** like chocolate decadence torte on a raspberry coulis

# Halfway House

A very Cypriot ambience; summer roof terrace with fine views. Turn up for lunch and an interesting selection of *mezes* will appear (see right), perhaps including *sigara böreği* with blue cheese, salad, chips and olives. Cypriot specialities may be available in high season, but otherwise telephone ahead, and the dish will be prepared for you.

**HALFWAY HOUSE**
**on the road between Karaman and Edremit ✆ (0533) 8657159 or (0392) 8223314 daily, lunch and dinner ££**

## *Zeytinli ekmek* (Olive bread)

Pre-heat the oven to 190° C. Lightly grease an 18 or 23 cm square cake tin.

Mix well together the eggs, olive oil, yoghurt, salt, mint & lemon. Fold in flour and olives, to make a very stiff mix, then bake, allowing 45-50min for the 18 cm tin and 35-40min for the 23 cm tin.

Ingredients

- 4 eggs
- 100 ml olive oil
- 100 g natural yoghurt
- 150 g black olives, stoned & chopped
- 450 g self-raising flour
- 1/8 tsp salt
- 1/4 tsp dried mint
- juice of 1/2 lemon

This recipe for olive bread is a personal addition, one we discovered when we lived in Turkey and were invited home for a typical Turkish tea. Sweet and savoury goodies were all placed on the table together, and everyone tucked in. This 'bread' is more like unsweetened cake. Eat it buttered or plain — or spread with *nor* or cottage cheese and honey for a yummy treat. Freezes well.

## *Zeytinyağli taze bakla* (Fresh broad beans in olive oil)

This is a popular dish when fresh young broad beans first appear and can be served with a yoghurt and garlic mix.

Mix the flour, water and lemon juice. In a pan, heat a little of the olive oil and soften the onion, then the spring onions, if used.

Remove from heat and add the beans, flour mix, salt and sugar. Bring to the boil, cover and simmer until tender and some liquid remains. Stir in half the dill and some pepper and leave to cool slightly. Serve garnished with more dill and a dribble of olive oil.

Ingredients (for 4 people)

- 500 g fresh young whole broad beans, washed
- 4 spring onions (optional)
- 1 medium. onion, chopped
- 300 ml water
- 70 ml olive oil
- 40 ml lemon juice
- 1 tbsp flour
- 1 tsp sugar
- 1/2 bunch dill, chopped
- salt & ground black pepper

## *Soğanli tavuk yahnisi* (Chicken with onions; *no photograph*)

This is a dish we've enjoyed at Tervetuloa (see page 66).

Sauté the chicken; set aside. Soften the onion in the juices. Add the flour and cook briefly, stirring, then add the chopped tomato and tomato paste and cook a further 1min. Add the water and vinegar; season to taste. Cover the pan and simmer about 20min, until the chicken is tender.

Ingredients (for 2 people)

- 500 g chicken joints or 2 chicken breasts, cut into bite size pieces
- 2 onions, chopped
- 1 large tomato, skinned & grated
- 1 tsp tomato paste
- 2 tbsp sunflower oil
- 1 tbsp flour
- 150 ml hot water
- 50 ml vinegar
- 1 chicken stock cube (dissolve in the hot water)
- 1/4 tsp cumin (either add to the recipe or sprinkle over the dish before serving)
- salt & black pepper to taste

## *Börülce* (Black-eyed beans)

Soak the beans in water overnight, then drain. Boil the beans gently in a large pan of water, which generously covers the beans, for around 1h. Add more water if needed. They are ready when they are soft but still firm. Be careful not to overcook or they will become mushy.

Drain, rinse with hot water and place in a bowl. Mix all the other ingredients with the beans and serve warm or cold. Reheats easily in the microwave.

Ingredients (for 4 people)

- 200 g black-eyed beans
- 1 garlic clove, crushed
- 3 tsp vinegar or red wine vinegar
- some chopped fresh parsley
- 25 g olive oil
- 2-3 spring onions, chopped or 1 red onion, finely sliced
- salt & black pepper

St Hilarion is often said to have inspired Walt Disney to dream up Snow White's castle and, as you approach it, you can really appreciate its fairy-tale character as it spirals up the peak. After your visit, a drive along the exhilarating ridge road is the prelude to lunch at a superbly sited restaurant.

# 3 st hilarion castle EXCURSION

**Distance:** only 52km/33mi, but the ridge road beyond St Hilarion is very narrow and slow driving *(note that this road will not suit nervous drivers or passengers)*. Allow half a day, but longer if you spend a lot of time at the castle and then follow the ridge road to Kozan Restaurant.

**Route:** Kyrenia — St Hilarion Castle — ridge road — Karşıyaka — Kyrenia

**Refreshments:** St Hilarion Castle, Kozan Restaurant

**Leave Kyrenia** by taking the road to Lefkoşa. As you near the top of the climb up the northern flanks of the Kyrenia Mountains, look for the right turn to St Hilarion Castle. The road winds still higher, passing through **militarised zones** *where you are requested not to stop, leave the car or take photographs.* Finally you turn right to climb the last steep hill to the castle — the route straight ahead at this point is the ridge road, followed in the next stage of the excursion.

There is a charge to enter **St Hilarion Castle** (open daily 08.00-18.00 in summer, 09.00-16.30 in winter; last admission one hour before closing). Exploring every nook and cranny in the castle will take some energy; it is built on three different levels on the mountain peak, so expect plenty of steps and steep uphills. Refreshments are available at the castle entrance and inside the castle as well.

St Hilarion takes its name from a monk who took refuge here after fleeing Palestine in the 7th century; he decided it was the perfect spot to become a hermit. Later a monastery was built on the site, and eventually that was fortified to protect it from Arab attacks. Along with the castles of Buffavento and Kantara, it formed a chain of defence along these northern mountains. St Hilarion was the last of these castles to fall to the Crusaders in 1191. The castle was greatly improved in Lusignan times, and during a fairly prolonged period of peace in the 13/14th century, it served as a summer palace.

The castle has **three main sections, all on different levels**. The lower section was built for soldiers and the castle workers. The climb up to the second level is not overly arduous; up here you can see the roofless **Byzantine chapel** and the **banqueting hall**, now a café/souvenir shop.

Steep steps then lead up to the final section which sprawls over this wild mountaintop. It is worth the climb to see the **royal apartments** from the Lusignan period, with their beautiful **Gothic windows**. The last challenge for many is to climb to the **western tower** and the **summit** (732m/1670ft); there are ample handrails.

Return down the castle access road and turn right at the bottom, to drive along the surfaced **ridge road**. Again

Gothic windows in the royal apartments at St Hilarion Castle

The tank, a bizarre 'tourist attraction'

there is a short stretch which is military, and *you are asked not to stop or take photographs.* There are only one or two places where you might wish to stop for a break or to look for flowers. Apart from the mountain scenery, there are views down to the southern plain one moment, then to the northern coast the next. Along one stretch there are prolonged views down onto the larger villages of Alsancak and Lapta.

Not too long after this stretch you arrive at **the tank**, a rather curious tourist attraction. Fortunately, there is room to stop. This army tank has been here since 1974. The tracks are still beside the road, but the tank is lodged partly over the slope. From here the road descends to a T-junction. The gates directly opposite lead into the grounds of the superbly located Kozan Restaurant (see page 85). If you feel like stretching your legs after the car journey, there are a couple of short walk possibilities from the restaurant grounds, described on page 84.

If you are not calling at the restaurant, turn right to continue downhill. The road winds and twists as it descends to the village of **Karşıyaka**. Keep left downhill as you approach the mosque, and turn left again at the T-junction opposite the abandoned Greek church. This leads down to the main coast road, where a right turn returns to Kyrenia in about 40 minutes.

# A walk and a climb from Kozan

There are two short options from Kozan — the first a gentle walk (1h), but the second climbs to the nearby mountaintop of 'Yurultulmus' (1h15min). This latter route is for more experienced walkers with agility; as the terrain is steep and rough, and some route-finding expertise is needed. *Note, too:* snakes are commonplace in rocky areas, so *be vigilant*. Take note of the route on the way uphill for the return. For equipment, see page 22.

**The start** of both options is the same: follow the woodland track continuing along the ridge from the restaurant. In around 5min, just before a **fountain** on the right, a path forks off right.

**For the walk**, fork right here. The path gradually descends around the contour, initially through forest but, as the trees thin out, views open out. Turn back as soon as the path becomes faint (about 15min-20min from the fork), and return uphill the same way. Unless you are experienced at route-finding do not go further.

**To climb to the summit**, stay ahead. The track narrows and continues round to the left. Soon, when it starts to descend, look for a path heading right, uphill, towards rocks. It's quite steep and slippery at the start. In a few minutes, the path leads uphill along the ridge towards a **red arrow** painted on a rock face. Clamber over rocks from here, following **red dots**, to rise onto the summit. *Note now where the path emerges onto the top, to locate it for your return.* Your reward is far-ranging panoramic views, as the mountain ridge diminishes towards Sadrazamköy, over Güzelyurt Bay and the Meseora Plain to the Troodos range in the south. Return, carefully, the same way.

Kozan

# Kozan (restaurant, café & picnic area)

A magnificent mountain location (see opposite), especially during the heat of summer, but idyllic any time. To get there from the main coast road, head into the centre of Karşıyaka and turn sharp right uphill just past the abandoned Greek church on the left (sign for 'Kozan'). At the top of the hill, where the ridge road goes left, turn right through black iron gates (closed when no one is there); the restaurant is ahead. Fork left towards the picnic area, to park beneath the trees.

The restaurant sits on a platform at the edge of the mountain, surrounded by greenery. Run by Savaş, a vet from the nearby village of Kozan, who sources most of the food there. He also keeps horses, and there is the opportunity to ride in summer.

For those who prefer a picnic, there are picnic tables set beneath a canopy of trees, each with its own barbecue (small charge); a black bin liner is provided for rubbish. Kozan's property is scrupulously clean — including the toilets (and woe betide anyone who dares leave litter!).

**KOZAN**
**Ridge road above Kozan village**
**( Savaş on (0533) 8457070**
**Apr-Oct 10.00-20.00 & some winter Sundays if the weather is fine; cl Mon £-££**

all **locally sourced organic** food — mainly **barbecues** (lamb chops, *şeftali, şiş kebaps*

***kleftiko*** only on Sundays

for a **light lunch**, an **omelette** or selection of ***mezes*** is adequate (includes yoghurt, cheese and olives from Kozan village, and other seasonal dishes — perhaps humus; beetroot; *favaş* (dried broad beans, cooked and mashed); cauliflower in oil; peas, apple & celery; tomato and cucumber salad, etc — accompanied by local bread. A plate of chips can also be added to the *meze* selection.



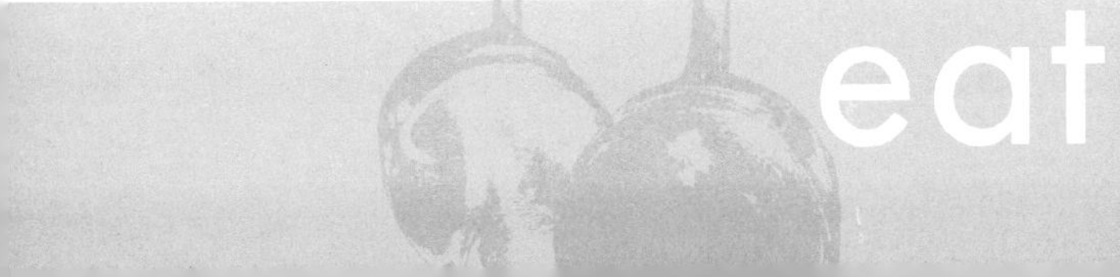

The impressive Gothic structure of Bellapais Abbey still dominates the landscape above Kyrenia despite encroaching habitation. Laurence Durrell would be hard-pressed to recognise the terrain he traversed in *Bitter Lemons*, but the old Crusader Way up from Ozanköy affords a glimpse of the grandeur of the past.

# 5 bellapais and ozanköy circuit WALK

**Distance:** 7km/4.4mi; 2h20min

**Grade:** moderate; mainly along tracks and sections of tarmac, with an overall height gain of 245m/800ft

**Equipment:** see page 22

**Transport:** 🚗 to Bellapais (see map on pages 28-29). Park in either of two car parks on entering Bellapais, preferably the second on the right, or at the car park just past the abbey

**Refreshments:** Plenty of choice in Bellapais, including Kahvehanasi ('Coffee House'; drinks) by the abbey ticket office, Azafran just along the road at the start of the walk (drinks/snacks), Paşa Pide, Bellapais Gardens and Kybele restaurants. Five Fingers Restaurant/Café in Ozanköy

**Alternative start:** Drive into Ozanköy and park near the mosque (limited parking). Walk ahead (east), past the Five Fingers Restaurant on the right, and pick up the notes at the 1h50min-point.

**Start the walk** from the **abbey entrance**: head inland, uphill, along the street opposite, **Bitter Lemons Street** (Hacı Limon Sokak), passing Azafran Café on the right. Keep ahead uphill to pass 'Bitter Lemons House' (No 15) on the left, then soon turn left into cobbled **Kemer Sokak**. Take shallow steps uphill under a narrow arch, then turn right between houses on a concrete path. This leads to more steps: bend left and then right, to meet a tarmac road. Go right, to continue uphill to another tarmac road, where you turn left. Pause here to enjoy fantastic views — towering limestone crags appear to block the route ahead, and an abandoned Greek church is amongst the trees to the right.

As the road makes a U-bend to the right and there is a small **old sentry post box** on the left (**20min**), go left on a track and start to descend, with more good views (but watch the stony track underfoot). This balcony track curves round the contours as it descends, and mandrake plants decorate the way in spring.

After 1.2km along the track you reach a junction: turn left, to pass a circular concrete **water tank** on the right. At the top of a rise (**50min**), go right, seaward, on a minor track, just before a **building** on the left. Initially, a concrete **water channel** runs alongside on the left and there is an almond grove on the right. Ignore a track joining from the left and notice another concrete **water tank** over to the right. The walk is now along a ridge, and the track crosses a point between two ravines and continues to wind downhill between valleys.

Descend to a T-junction and turn left; mandrakes and cyclamen flourish here in March. After 200m, at the next junction, turn right to dip across the valley bottom and immediately rise to a further junction. Stay ahead (left) uphill; at the top of the rise the track becomes tarmac. When you meet the tarmac road coming from Bellapais, turn right downhill. At a steep concrete section, the **Crusader Way** can be seen below to the left. Pass the point where it begins (almost opposite house No 31; **1h30min**) and continue downhill into **Ozanköy**. Follow the main road round to the left (where Erol's restaurant is to the right). Behind the intriguing blue door in the wall on the left is the medieval church of **Panayía Potamítissa**, which has been restored by a Turkish Cypriot resident. A local often appears and offers to get the key (if not, ask Alex at Five Fingers). Inside are remains of frescoes which once covered the walls, the frame of a decorated wooden iconstasis, and a 14th century engraved tomb. At the next junction, notice a small ***hammam*** (Turkish bath, now a storage shed) on the left, tucked against the wall below the church. Follow the road as it curves right, then turn left, to pass the **Five Fingers Restaurant** on the left (**1h45min**). Then stay ahead to reach the **mosque** and village square in a couple of minutes.

Iconstasis in Panayía Potamítissa

Walk back to the 1h30min-point. Where the road bends left, stay ahead on the track, to take the **Crusader Way**. Follow this track as it loops in an S before starting uphill towards Bellapais, with a valley on the right. Some illegal bulldozing has widened out a section of track just before you emerge in the grounds of the **Bellapais Gardens Hotel**, through which the route passes beneath the walls of the abbey. The hotel restaurant is the last building on the right before you reach steps leading left uphill — straight back to **Bellapais centre** and the **Kybele** restaurant. Or stay ahead for Paşa Pide restaurant (evenings only out of season); it's on the main road almost opposite the exit from the Crusader Way. Turn left uphill back to **Bellapais Abbey** (**2h20min**).

# Bellapais Gardens Hotel & Restaurant

Matchless service and a wonderful location, with views down to the coast from the restaurant. A relaxed, welcoming atmosphere and superb food and drink — the ideal venue for that special occasion. It is also a great, homely place to stay. To find this gem,

**BELLAPAIS GARDENS**
**at the top of the Crusader Way in Bellapais ✆ (0392) 8157668**
**daily for drinks, lunch and dinner; book for evening meals £££**

classic menu with plenty of choice

**starters** include traditional lamb's liver sauté, chef's special pastry roll

**salads**: Bellapais artichoke salad, Cyprus salad, caesar salad

various local **meats,** like steaks with different sauces (mustard & honey, brandy), **grills** like *şeftali kebap*, lamb bon fillet, rack of lamb

traditional Cypriot ***stifado***

**fish** – swordfish, sea bream, bass

**pasta** with salmon or pesto sauce;

**desserts** from a self-service array

The authors (top left and bottom right) enjoy a 'special occasion' dinner with friends at Bellapais.

head into Bellapais village. Turn left into a narrow signposted road almost opposite the Paşa Pide Restaurant on the right. This is the start of the Crusader Way, and the restaurant is the first building on the left, a little way downhill below the abbey walls.

# Kybele Bar & Restaurant

There are sweeping views down to the coast from this restaurant with plenty of choice — and the setting beside the abbey walls couldn't be more spectacular (see photograph on page 88).

**KYBELE BAR/RESTAURANT**
**in the grounds of Bellapais Abbey**
**☏ (0392) 8157531-33**
**daily, from 00.00-00.00 ££**

extensive menu of **drinks**, **snacks** and **main meals**

**FIVE FINGERS**
**in the centre of Ozanköy ☏ (0533) 88458278 or (0392) 8152010**
**daily, from 11.00-15.00 and from 18.00 'till late' ££**

English **breakfast**

**snacks**, **sandwiches**, **salads**, **omelettes**

choice of 15 **pizzas**

substantial **evening menu**

A relaxed ambience at Five Fingers

# Five Fingers Restaurant & Café/Bar

A homespun atmosphere in a village building which also houses The Garden Bookshop (new & used books), so diners can browse the shelves while they wait. There is the option of sitting in the sheltered courtyard or on the roof terrace with its excellent view of Bellapais Abbey. The homemade lemonade is delicious. Some dishes on the evening menu have a 'Turkish twist', with options for children, and food is freshly prepared.

## *Kiliç* (Swordfish)

Wash and dry the steaks and place in a shallow dish. Mix the marinade ingredients and pour over (make sure the steaks are well coated). Cover and leave in the fridge for a few hours or at least 30min.

Heat the grill to medium-high. Drain the fish and grill for 5min each side at most. If the steaks are thin, allow less cooking time or the fish will become dry.

Ingredients (for 2 people)

2 (150 g) swordfish steaks (fresh preferably)

*For the marinade*

1 tbsp olive oil
70 ml lemon juice
25 g plain yoghurt
1/4 tsp dried dill or 1/2 tbsp fresh dill, chopped
1 tsp dried mint or 1 tbsp fresh mint, chopped
1 garlic clove, pressed
salt & black pepper

## *Cacık (no photograph)*

A 'must' with meals — whether you're having a simple wrap or restaurant *meze*. *Cacık* is often thinned with a little water and served like a cold soup. On mainland Turkey it's served as a side dish, alongside the main meal.

Ingredients (for 4 servings)

2-3 cucumbers, grated or chopped finely
2-3 garlic cloves, crushed or grated
500 g plain yoghurt
olive oil
salt & pepper
fresh dill, chopped (optional)

Squeeze as much liquid as possible out of the cucumber and mix well with the yoghurt. Add the garlic to taste, a touch of olive oil, salt & pepper and the dill, if used. Taste as you go!

## *Stifado*

Lamb is the traditional meat for this dish, but beef is commonly used instead. In North Cyprus onions are used instead of shallots. Vinegar is also a feature of many Cypriot dishes.

Ingredients (for 2 people)

- 400 g stewing steak cut into 4cm/1.5in chunks
- 1 tbsp olive oil
- 1 level tbsp flour
- 1 large onion, sliced
- 1 garlic clove, crushed
- 150 ml red wine (or Cyprus Commanderia wine)
- 1 beef stock cube
- 50 ml water
- 20 ml vinegar
- 2 bay leaves
- 1/4 tsp cinnamon
- 1/4 tsp cloves powder
- 1 tsp dark soya sauce
- 1 tsp worcester sauce
- 1/2 tsp dried oregano (optional)
- salt & black pepper to taste

Preheat the oven to 170-180° C. Toss the meat in seasoned flour. Heat the oil in a frying pan and brown the meat, then remove with a slotted spoon to a casserole dish.

Caramelise the onions in the frying pan (without burning), to give colour, then add the garlic, spices, soya sauce, worcester sauce, stock cube, water, vinegar and wine. Bring to the boil, stirring, then pour over the meat in the casserole.

Cook for about 2h, until the meat is tender. Add extra water, if needed, part way through cooking.

There are many variations on a theme with mousaka recipes, but all basically contain the same ingredients. It's a matter of inclination as to how they are put together. In Cyprus the dish usually contains only aubergine or potato, not both. But anything goes, and flavourings play an important part. The recipe below can easily be adjusted for any number of people. Even the topping can be a straightforward white sauce with cheese, a béchamel sauce or one containing egg yolk.

*Frying* the aubergines or potatoes can turn this into a very oily (though very tasty) dish. But the aubergine slices can be brushed with oil and baked or dry-fried. Eileen's long-used method is to layer the sliced aubergine in a dish, drizzling a little oil over each layer. Cover with clingfilm and microwave until soft, around 8-10min, or par boil potatoes 15min. It doesn't appear to make any difference to the finished flavour and is far less oily.

## Alex's aubergine mousaka

This recipe comes from Alex, proprietor of the Five Fingers Restaurant. Preheat the oven to 200° C. Cook the onion in butter until golden, add the meat and cook, stirring, 5min. Add stock cube, water, plus 2 chopped tomatoes. Simmer 20min in and open pan. Prepare the aubergines; either fry, bake or microwave.

In a buttered dish, make a layer of half the aubergines. Spread the meat over the top, then cover with the rest of the aubergines. Top with 3 sliced tomatoes.

For the sauce, make a roux with the flour and butter by melting the butter and combining with the flour then, using a balloon whisk, gradually add the milk and seasoning. Continue to stir over the heat until the mixture boils and thickens. (If using a microwave, melt the butter, then add the flour using a balloon whisk to combine the two.

Cook 30 seconds, then gradually whisk in the milk and seasoning. Microwave on high for 2min, stir, then continue in 1min bursts, stirring in between until the sauce bubbles and thickens. Watch carefully, to prevent the mixture boiling over.)

Spread the sauce over the mixture in the dish, sprinkle with grated cheese, and bake for about 20-25min, until brown on top.

*Alternative toppings:* For a plain sauce, we omit the nutmeg and bay leaves from the ingredients listed. Or we make a plain sauce (as above), seasoned with salt & pepper, then stir in 1 egg yolk and 60 g of grated cheese. Spread the sauce over the mixture in the dish and sprinkle over some grated cheese. While Alex uses a higher setting of 200° C, we bake our mousakas at 180°C for 30-40 min until brown on top.

Mousaka can be frozen for a few weeks or left overnight on the chiller tray in the fridge, which will enhance the flavour.

Ingredients (for 4 people)

6 medium size aubergines
2 small onions, chopped
250 g minced lamb
1 lamb stock cube (or chicken)
200 ml water
100 g grated *helim* or cheddar cheese
5 medium tomatoes (2 of them chopped)
butter and sunflower oil for frying
béchamel sauce for the topping

*For the béchamel sauce*

600 ml milk
2 tbsp flour
60 g butter
1/2 tsp nutmeg (optional)
2 bay leaves (optional)
black pepper

Two walks in one day's outing: you round the perimeter of the famous Five Finger Mountain, after which the whole Kyrenia range is named, and tackle an exhilarating climb to the dramatic pinnacle fortress of Buffavento Castle. This challenging but rewarding excursion can be spread over two days.

# beşparmak circuit and buffavento

# WALK 6

**Distance:** 5.5km/4.3mi; 1h50min for the circuit;45min for the castle

**Grade:** moderate track walk on the circuit, with an overall height gain of 110m/360ft; height gain of 160m/525ft on the stepped footpath to Buffavento Castle

**Equipment:** see page 22

**Transport:** 🚗 to Buffavento Restaurant at the top of Beşparmak Pass (see map on pages 28-29). Adjacent to the restaurant, turn east on the narrow mountain road towards Alevkaya; 1.3km along fork left downhill on a track and park in an abandoned quarry. Alternatively, there is space to park off the road before descending and walk down the track to the start the circuit. After the circular walk, drive on to Buffavento Castle: return to Buffavento Restaurant, cross the main road with care, and stay right on a narrow mountain road. Turn right after 6km, then park below the castle.

**Refreshments:** Buffavento Restaurant (meals, snacks and drinks)

**Start the Beşparmak circuit** from the **quarry**: walk downhill on a rough track heading seawards. Meet a crossing track and turn right. Under 200m further on, turn sharp left downhill (**8min**). The pile of stones ahead at this point is the ruin of an **old lime kiln**. A track comes up sharply from the right to join yours, as you round the **Five Finger Mountain *(Beşparmak)***, with the sea over to the right. Views open out along the coast as the descending track curls beneath the mountain, first moving further away to the right, then back to the left.

On reaching a T-junction, go left and start into an ascent — quite steep initially, then briefly levelling out (good views far up the coast to the west are excuse enough to pause for a breather). Continue to rise on a more gentle gradient towards the saddle ahead. Just before reaching the top of the saddle, a minor track enters from the right. If you're planning to picnic, the area here is as good a spot as any on the route. Take

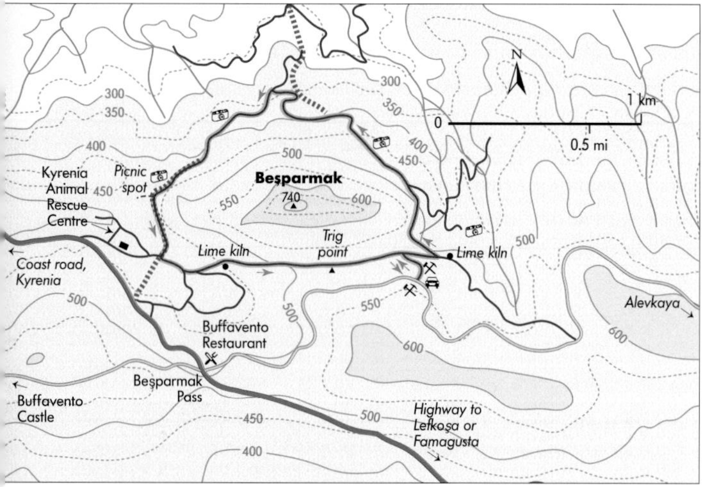


care if you decide to explore the caves in the rocky terrain on the right.

Once on **the saddle**, the Kyrenia Animal Rescue Centre comes into view over to the right (but barking dogs may have alerted you to it before you see it). Descend to a T-junction and turn left (right leads to the Animal Rescue Centre). Pass a wide track on the right and enjoy a fairly level section along the valley bottom. You can see Buffavento Restaurant above, over to the right. Ignore a track forking right just before the track you are on rises. Pass another **old lime kiln** on the right and reach a saddle. A **trig point** marks a high point, beyond which the track starts to descend. After about 250m, meet your outward track and fork right uphill, back to the **quarry** (**1h50min**).

For the second part of the outing, drive on to **Buffavento Castle** and take the stepped footpath out of the car park. Timings for the climb can vary enormously, but it takes us 20-25 minutes at a steady pace to reach the top. There is no entry charge, but take care when exploring the ruins. This castle is the highest of the castles along the Kyrenia mountain range, at 940m (3085ft), and offers fantastic views as far as the eye can see.

Buffavento castle, and the far-reaching view from the top

# Buffavento Restaurant

Enjoy the best view of Beşparmak Mountain from this very Turkish-style restaurant. Dine outside in summer on a covered verandah and, for a traditional Turkish experience, book the raised platform and sit on cushions round a low circular table.

Inside the restaurant, and their huge *meze* selection (right) — with a somewhat overflowing bread basket

**BUFFAVENTO RESTAURANT**
**Beşparmak Pass ( (0533) 8645388**
**daily from about 11.00-23.00 ££**

**kebab house** with a large selection of ***mezes*** and a choice of lamb or chicken ***şiş kebaps***

***adana kebaps*** or **lamb chops** in the evening

daytime **snacks** and lighter meals

## *Etli nohut* (Chickpea stew)

Preheat the oven to 170° C.

Dust the meat in seasoned flour and brown in the olive oil. Set the meat aside on a plate. Soften the onion and garlic in the pan. Stir in the tomato paste, dried oregano, chopped tomato and salt & pepper.

Bring to the boil and add the browned meat. Re-heat and add extra water if needed. Place in a casserole and cook for about 1h.

Remove the casserole from the oven, stir in the chickpeas and return to the oven for a further 20min.

*Alternatively:* This recipe also works well in a wine-based sauce with pork. Omit the tin of tomatoes and replace it with 200 ml of white wine. Add 1 tbsp flour mixed with white wine when the chickpeas are added.

Ingredients (for 4 people)

400 g cooked chickpeas or 2 x 425 g tin drained
1 kg cubed pork or beef
2 medium onions, chopped
2 garlic cloves, crushed
2 x 400 g tin chopped tomatoes
2 tbsp tomato paste
250 ml stock (chicken or beef)
1 tsp dried oregano
3 tbsp fresh parsley, chopped
1 tsp cumin (optional)
4 tbsp olive oil
salt & pepper

## *Karnıyarık* (Aubergines stuffed with mince)

Preheat the oven to 180° C. If the aubergines are fat and round, slice in half. For long, thin aubergines, peel a 1 cm strip lengthwise, then a smaller strip across the middle, to make a cross. After frying, slit to form a pouch.

Fry the aubergines all over in the sunflower oil until pale golden (but do not burn).Fry the peppers. Drain both on absorbent paper. Soften the onion in oil or butter; add the meat and brown. Stir in all the other stuffing ingredients, cover, and cook gently 20-30min. The mixture needs to be fairly dry. (When using fat round aubergines, scoop a little flesh out of the halved pieces and cook with the filling mix.)

Pack the aubergines in an oven dish, just large enough to hold them together. Divide the filling and pile onto the half pieces or fill the pouch openings on the long, thin aubergines. Decorate with a pepper and a slice of tomato.

Dilute the tomato paste in 200 ml of hot water and pour into the base of the dish. Cover with foil and bake about 25min. Remove the foil halfway through cooking.

Ingredients (for 4 people):

4 aubergines (long thin) or 2 large (round)
75 ml sunflower oil for frying
1 large tomato, sliced (garnish)
4 small light green, sweet peppers *(çarliston biber)*
1 tbsp tomato paste (for the cooking liquid)

*For the filling*

250 g minced lamb or beef (finely ground if beef)
20 g butter
1 onion, grated (or can use 2 tsp minced garlic paste)
1/2 bunch fresh parsley, finely chopped)
2 large tomatoes, skinned and finely chopped or 1 x 400 g tin of chopped tomatoes
200 ml water (omit if using tinned tomatoes)
salt & pepper to taste

## *Kırmısı mercimek çorbası* (Red lentil soup; *not illustrated*)

Lightly fry the onions and garlic. Add the cumin and paprika. Wash the lentils, add to the pan and fry 2min. Add stock and tomato paste. Bring to the boil and simmer until the lentils are soft, about 20min, then add salt & pepper to taste. If you like it spicy, a touch of *acı biber* (hot pepper powder) could be added. Blend the soup, and serve with lemon wedges and your chosen garnish.

For a thicker soup, add either 1/2 cup of bulgar wheat, couscous, cooked rice or cooked potato (1 potato could be added to cook with the soup).

Ingredients (for 4 people — or 2 people for lunch)

1 medium. onion, chopped)
1 garlic clove, crushed
150 g red lentils
1 tsp cumin
1 tsp paprika
1 tbsp tomato paste
600 ml veg/chicken stock (2 cubes)
salt & pepper to taste
lemon juice & parsley or fresh coriander or mint (garnish)

## *Sütlaç* (Turkish rice pudding; *photograph on page 111*)

Add water to rice in a pan; bring to the boil. Simmer gently in an open pan, stirring occasionally, until the water is absorbed and the rice is soft. Add the milk and bring to boil, stirring. Simmer uncovered 30min, stirring frequently, to avoid a skin forming. Add sugar and stir to dissolve, then add the cornflour, mixed with a little milk. Finally, add the vanilla essence. Simmer a further 10min to thicken. Pour into individual bowls.

Traditionally served cold, sprinkled with cinnamon — equally delicious warm.

Ingredients (for 4 people)

100 g rice (short-grain, risotto or arborio)
400 ml water
1 litre full cream milk
50 g sugar
20 g cornflour *(nişasta)*
1 tsp vanilla essence or rose water to taste
cinnamon

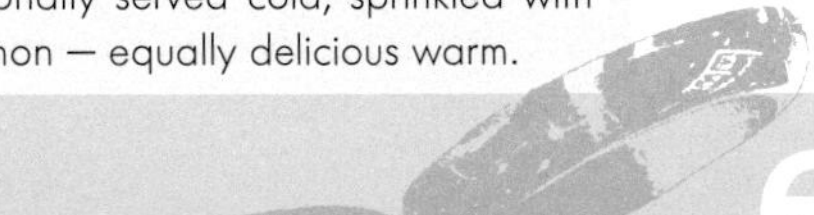

This forest walk traverses both the north and south sides of the Beşparmak range. Highlights include the viewpoint at 'Lover's Leap', a 'forest' of strawberry trees, a wealth of springtime flowers and the ruins of Sourp Magar, an early Christian monastery.

# 7 sourp magar circuit WALK

**Distance:** 6.7km/4.2mi; 2h15min

**Grade:** moderate, on tracks and paths, with an overall height gain of 170m/557ft. Occasional blue waymarks indicate the route but do not rely solely on them.

**Equipment:** see page 22

**Transport:** 🚗 to Buffavento Restaurant at the top of the Beşparmak Pass (see map on pages 28-29). Then continue east along the narrow ridge road (passing places) to a large picnic site, 7.9km from the restaurant. The North Cyprus Herbarium at Alevkaya, a mecca for botanists, is nearby: to visit it, turn right at the junction soon reached — it's a short way along, on the left, at Alevkaya Forest Station (another picnic area; café/restaurant). A left turn at this junction leads to Esentepe (for our recommended restaurants) and the coastal road — for a possible swim at Alagadi (Turtle Bay).

**Refreshments:** Buffavento Restaurant (see page 100); Hati's and Zırdeli in Esentepe

**The walk starts** from the **picnic site**: walk back, west, along the road. In a little over a minute, two almost-adjacent tracks turn off left. The first heads downhill, but take the second track, which rises; there are **blue dots** at the start. Glimpses of Alevkaya Forest Station over to the left are caught through the trees, before the track swings west along the south side of the Beşparmak Mountains. You enjoy a good outlook over the Meseora Plain stretching south into the distance.

Just 1km along the track, at a junction (**25min**), go right, then bend left uphill. The track levels out in pine woods and reaches a clearing with a **red/blue waymarked concrete pillar**. Stay ahead along the grassy track, ignoring tracks off to the left. Pass a **red/blue waymarked rock** on the left and start to descend on a minor track which reverts to a path through limestone. More views open up before the path swings back in a more northerly

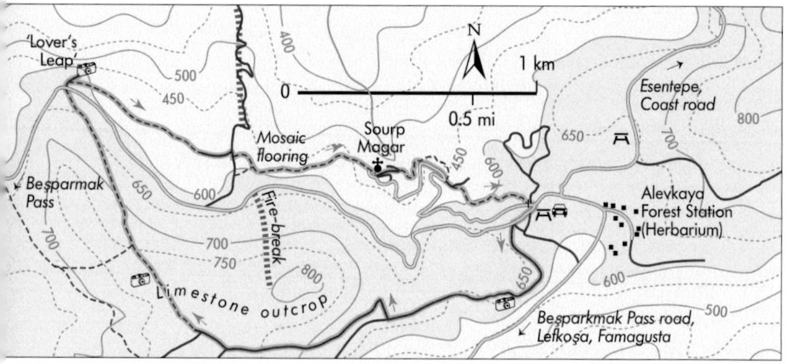


direction. Where a path rises from the left to join the one you are on (by a large **limestone outcrop**), keep ahead — as indicated by a **blue arrow** on a rock. The path descends on the north side of the ridge and swings west along its flanks. *Take care on this descent,* which can be slippery after rain. Reach the **ridge road** and cross to the **viewpoint** known locally as **'Lover's Leap'**(**1h10min**).

To continue, take the pleasant woodland path descending east, just 10m north of the road. It joins a minor track, then rises to a crossing track. Turn right briefly, then go left on a path which soon bends right and rises to a crossing path — and the remains of **mosaic flooring**, indicating that there was once some habitation in this area. Continue left along what becomes a high-level mountainside path through a forest of **strawberry trees** *(Arbutus andrachne)*. The ruins of Sourp Magar come into view below, cradled in a secluded bowl at the head of a ravine. For the easiest descent to the monastery, keep left across a bit of concrete, then head down to the right and straight on.

**Sourp Magar** (**St Makarios**; **1h50min**), originally founded in 1000AD by Coptic Christians from Alexandria in Egypt, came into the hands of Armenians during the 15th century. It was a favoured stop-off spot for pilgrims en route to the Holy Land and, even though the last monks left in the early 20th century, it remained a favoured place for Armenian families to visit until 1974. Explore the monastery and perhaps even picnic there, but take great care, as much of the structure is unsafe.

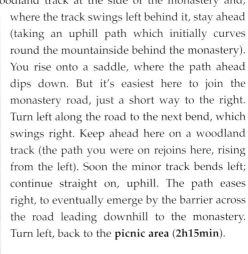

The road from the monastery returns to the start of the walk, but is twice as long; the path is preferable. To locate the path, go down the woodland track at the side of the monastery and, where the track swings left behind it, stay ahead (taking an uphill path which initially curves round the mountainside behind the monastery). You rise onto a saddle, where the path ahead dips down. But it's easiest here to join the monastery road, just a short way to the right. Turn left along the road to the next bend, which swings right. Keep ahead here on a woodland track (the path you were on rejoins here, rising from the left). Soon the minor track bends left; continue straight on, uphill. The path eases right, to eventually emerge by the barrier across the road leading downhill to the monastery. Turn left, back to the **picnic area** (**2h15min**).

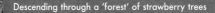

Descending through a 'forest' of strawberry trees

# Hati's Café/Bar Restaurant

A delightful backwater, tucked away on the edge of Esentepe, where you can unwind and enjoy some excellent food. Hatıce (who speaks good English) loves cooking and likes to serve her food fresh, *not* out of the freezer. She will happily prepare Cypriot/Turkish dishes and her delicious *sütlaç* on request. So if you want a substantial meal, telephone before setting out.

To get there, head for the centre of Esentepe. *Approaching from the coast* road, drive up into the village and turn left just before 'Kim Market'; follow this road round to the right, to the end of the road. *Approaching from the mountains*, stay ahead as you reach the centre into Dedirman Sokak (where the main road is signposted round to the left). At the T-junction, turn right to the end of the road; Hati's is on the left.

**HATI'S CAFÉ/BAR RESTAURANT**
**Esentepe ☎ (0533) 8633862**
**daily for breakfast, lunch and dinner; cl Sun until 20.00 ££**

**snacks** and **light meals** – hamburgers, toast, omelettes and kebabs are always available

**Cypriot meals** only to order – check in advance.

# Zırdeli Café/Bar

A restaurant with a difference — a tented structure with gravel floor and a green garden oasis behind for hot summer days. The tent is heated in winter. Rustic, Cypriot, friendly, and very clean — with good food.

Look for the 'tent' on the left as you are entering Esentepe from the mountains or, if approaching from the coast, on the right — after driving through the village, past the mosque.

The green garden oasis outside Zırdeli

**ZIRDELİ CAFÉ/BAR**
**in the centre of Esentepe**
**( (0533) 8445340/ 8430186; daily from 18.00-01.00 in winter; 13.00-01.00 in summer**
**££**

all meals served with 7 ***mezes***

chicken or lamb ***şiş kebaps***, chicken or lamb chops, roast chicken and roast beef, lamb or chicken ***kleftiko***

**Cypriot meals** only to order — check in advance.

### *Fırın makarna* (Baked macaroni with mince)

Pre-heat the oven to 180° C and start by making the meat sauce. Soften the chopped onion in the olive oil, then add the meat to brown. Keep stirring until the excess liquid evaporates. Stir in the garlic and the parsley.

Now, if you are not adding more ingredients, put to one side. **(Additional ingredients could include: 1 tbsp tomato paste and 150 ml red wine — or a veg/chicken/lamb stock cube dissolved in the wine or water.)** If you *are* using tomato paste, wine/water and a stock cube, add them at this point and bring to the boil. Simmer gently, uncovered, for 20min — adding the fresh parsley 10min into simmering time.

Meanwhile, bring a large pan of water to the boil with a pinch of salt and few drops of vegetable or olive oil. Cook the *makarna* for about 9min, and drain.

Ingredients (for 4 people)

*For the meat sauce*

- 500 g minced lamb/beef
- 2 medium onions, chopped or grated
- 2 garlic cloves, crushed or grated, or 2 tsp minced garlic
- 1/2 bunch fresh parsley, finely chopped, or 1 heaped tsp of dry
- 2 tbsp olive oil
- salt & pepper to taste

*For the pasta*

- 200-250g *makarna* (macaroni) pasta (the pasta sold in the longer, fat tubes works best — look for word *'firin'* on the packet); 200 g is usually enough, but for hearty appetites use 250 g

*For the sauce (or cream as it is called locally)*

- 500 ml milk
- 2 heaped tbsp flour
- 50 g butter
- 2 eggs, beaten slightly
- 2 drops of vanilla essence (optional)
- grated *helim* or cheddar cheese for the topping

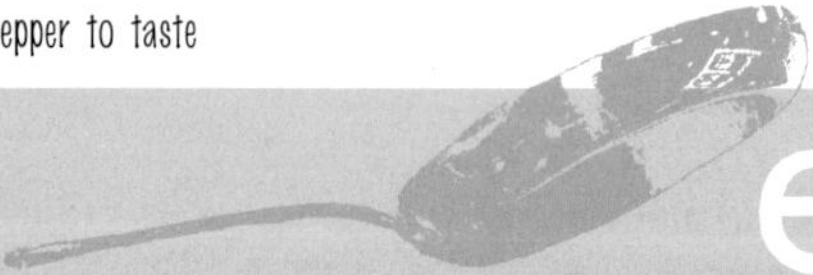

recipes

eat

*Fırın makarna* at Hati's – just one of several recipes Hatıce shared with us

While the pasta is cooking prepare the sauce. Make a roux by melting the butter in a pan. Take off the heat and blend in the flour. Heat gently to cook the flour. Remove from the heat and slowly add the milk (a whisk is useful here). Add the salt & pepper and bring to the boil, stirring constantly. The sauce needs to be quite thick. Take off the heat and cool slightly, then add the beaten egg a little at a time, as the sauce needs to be a thick custard-like consistency. Hatıce adds the vanilla essence at this point. (You could make the sauce in a microwave if there is one to hand, using the method described for the mousaka sauce described on page 94.)

Grease a large casserole, or a tin with high sides. Put half the makarna in the bottom and mix in a few spoonfuls of sauce. Add the meat layer then layer the remaining *makarna,* which has been mixed with a little sauce, and pour over the remaining sauce. Sprinkle grated *helim* or cheddar cheese on the top. Bake for about 30min or until it is brown on top. (Mixing a little sauce with the *makarna,* as Hatıce does, helps bind and moisturise.)

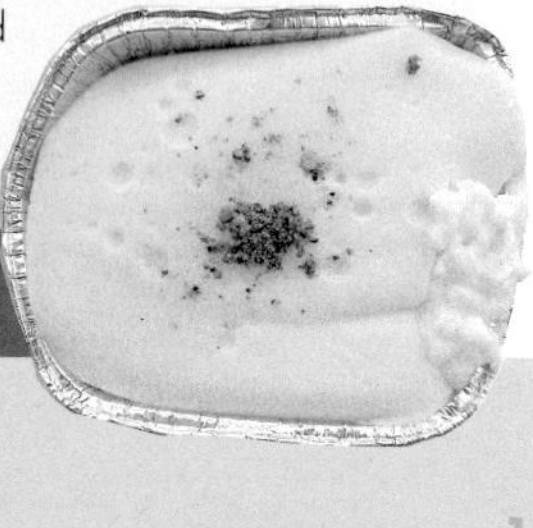

Another of Hatıce's specialities is *sütlaç;* *we took some away in a 'doggie bag'.*

## Hati's aubergine mousaka

This is a sauce- (cream-) free aubergine mousaka which is delicious and complements the *makarna* dish on page 111. Preheat the oven to 180° C.

Soften the onion in a pan, then add the garlic, dried parsley (if using) and mince. Brown the mince and cook, stirring, to remove the excess liquid, then add the fresh parsley, pepper and salt to taste.

Soften the aubergine slices, as in the mousaka recipe on page 94.

Grease a large casserole dish or tin. Place the mince mixture in the base, then layer the aubergines and top with slices of tomato. Cover with foil and put in the oven for 40-50min. Remove the foil after 25-30min.

Hatıce's sauce-free mousaka

Ingredients (for 4 people)

- 4 small or 2 large aubergines, sliced
- 2-3 medium onions, chopped (Hatıce loves loads of onions)
- 2 garlic cloves, crushed or grated
- 500 g minced lamb or beef
- 2 tbsp olive oil
- 4 tomatoes, sliced
- 1/2 bunch fresh parsley, finely chopped, or 1 tsp dried parsley (optional)
- salt & black pepper

## *Bulgar vermicelli pilav* (Cracked wheat and vermicelli); *not shown*

A Cypriot dish which can be made with rice in place of the bulgar wheat, just cook a little longer; it is eaten with fish, meat stews like *stifado,* and even as part of a *meze.* It's a lot tastier than it looks. See recipe and ingredients opposite.

Soften the onion in olive oil or butter then add the vermicelli and stir-fry gently 5-10min, until it's a pale gold colour. Add stock, bulgar or rice and seasoning. Cover the pan and simmer gently for around 15-20min, or until the liquid has been absorbed. Rice may need a little extra cooking and water. The mixture has to be *dry*. If using immediately, let it stand a few minutes. Fluff up the grains before serving. Can be chilled and reheated, when it might need a little extra water.

Ingredients (for 4-6 people)

125 ml olive oil or 50 g butter
1 medium onion, finely chopped
60 g vermicelli
400 g bulgar or rice
900 ml chicken stock (1 stock cube)
salt & black pepper (less salt if using a stock cube)

## Humus *(not illustrated)*

It's easy to use a can of chickpeas, but dried are better. This is the way we make it at home. Store covered in the fridge; it keeps a few days.

Soak the chickpeas overnight in water. Drain, put in a large pan and cover with water to about 4-5cm (1 inch) above the peas. Bring to the boil, then lower the heat, cover loosely to allow steam to escape, and boil gently for 1h to 1h15min, or until soft. Drain and reserve the water.

Put the chick peas and the rest of the ingredients in a bowl, reserving a little lemon juice and garlic, and blend. Taste, adding the rest of the lemon juice and garlic and more tahine, if wanted. If the mix is too stiff, add some of the drained cooking water until a satisfactory consistency is reached. The humus can be left fairly coarse or processed longer for a smoother mix. Add a touch of cumin or black pepper if you like.

Ingredients (for 4 people)

125 g dried chickpeas
100 g tahine (sesame seed paste, sold in jars in supermarkets)
1 large lemon (juice of)
3-4 garlic cloves, crushed, or 2-3 tsp minced garlic paste
cumin (optional)
black pepper (optional)

# 8

A delightful panoramic balcony walk which snakes around the contours, with the added interest of flowers in spring. The goal is the twelfth-century Byzantine monastery of Antiphonitis (Christ Who Responds) secreted amongst the folds of the mountain.

# antiphonitis WALK

**Start out** by heading east along the **signposted track**. This is a really relaxing walk along a stabilised track, ignoring tracks off left and right. At a bend (**35min**) you can't fail to notice a prominent rock on the left; we call it 'Camel Rock'. Pass a **trig point** on the left; then, curving into another valley, head for an electricity box, round **water tank** (1971) and water **fountain**. The tarmac road below is the monastery road from Esentepe, passed earlier. Meet this road (**1h10min**) and cross it diagonally, to head downhill. Glimpses of the monastery through the trees on the right present some good photographic opportunities.

There is a small entry fee to visit **Antiphonitis Monastery** (**1h20min**). Frescoes once completely adorned the interior, but a scattering still

**Distance:** 8.7km/5.5mi; 3h

**Grade:** easy-moderate out and back walk along tracks and a road, with an overall height gain of 100m/330ft on the return

**Equipment:** see page 22

**Transport:** 🚗 to Esentepe (see map on pages 28-29). Head inland through the village towards Alevkaya Forest Station. On leaving Esentepe, you pass a road off left signposted to Antiphonitis, but *keep ahead* and, in a further 2.8km, park by a track leading left off the road, signposted to 'Andifonitis 4km/Tirmen Boğaz 4km'. (Or, from the junction east of the picnic site at the start of Walk 7, turn left for Esentepe. Ignore the left fork to Karaağaç, and in 8.6km look for the signposted track as above, on your *right*.)

**Refreshments:** soft drinks/snacks at Antiphonitis; Hati's and Zırdeli in Esentepe (see pages 108-9); Alagadi Turtle Beach Restaurant; three restaurants in Alagadi village (the next bay west): Benöz (1st on the right), Hoca (2nd on the left), and the more rustic St Kathleen's nearer the coast

**Shorter walk:** 6.9km/4.3mi; 2h20min. Walk as far as the track/road junction, before the descent to the monastery, then return.

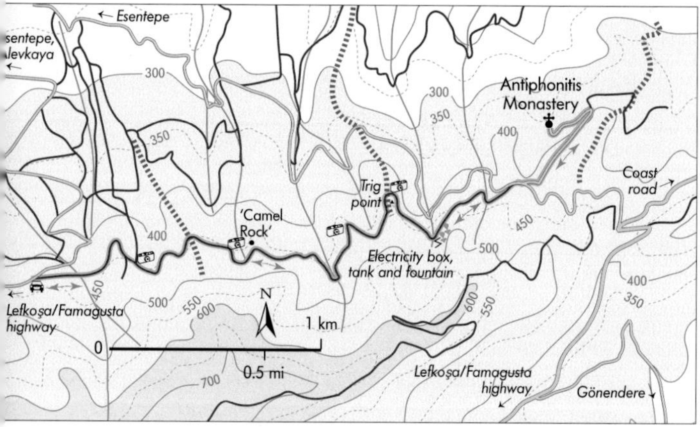


remain, with 'Christ Pantokrator' (a regular feature in domed churches) the most dominant. The friendly custodian sells drinks and biscuits. He is particularly proud of the special Cyprus endemic orchid *(Ophrys kotschyi),* which grows in the grounds. In springtime, he carefully nurtures the plants and tries to protect them from the footprints of unthinking visitors, but will happily show them off if asked. *(It is an offence to pick wild orchids.)*

To return, just retrace your outward route to the **track junction** (**3h**).

If you're after a meal now, an alternative if you're heading to the beach after this walk or Walk 7, all of the following are located in Alagadi village, 3km east of Acapulco Holiday Village. We recommend **Benöz** (0533) 8633823, with its shaded outdoor area and extensive fish menu (££); **Hoca** (0533)

8612506/ 8673517 has a pleasant terrace with views to the sea — mainly fish but also Turkish cuisine (££); **St Kathleen's** (0533) 8617640, is a little further along — at the fork where the road divides, on the left, towards the beach (*mezes*; *kebaps*; Cypriot dishes (££). All are open daily.

## *Etli biber dolma* (Stuffed peppers, *not illustrated*)

This recipe comes from Ebru, one of our Turkish friends in North Cyprus. It's quick and easy. Allow 2 peppers per person for a main meal.

Mix all the main ingredients well. Slice the tops off the peppers and remove the seeds. Stuff the peppers with the rice mix and replace the tops. Place tightly in a pan (if they are not packed together they will collapse). Top with slices of the extra tomatoes.

Mix the extra 2 tbsp tomato paste with some hot water and a little salt. Pour over the peppers in the pan and add more water to half fill the pan. Place small dabs of butter on the peppers. Cover the pan and leave on a low heat for about 1h.

Ingredients (for 4 people as a starter)

4 large peppers
1 large onion, grated
250 g minced lamb
150 g uncooked short-grain or risotto rice (100 g if the peppers are not very large)
2 large tomatoes, skinned and grated
1 tbsp tomato paste
1 bunch fresh parsley, finely chopped
salt & black pepper

*Cooking ingredients*

2 tomatoes
2 tbsp tomato paste
butter
salt

## *Ispanak böreği* (Spinach pie)

We've enjoyed some very moreish versions of this classic over the years. Be prepared to experiment with herb combinations, etc. Beaten egg is also sometimes added. If using frozen spinach, make sure you squeeze out as much moisture as possible before adding it to the pan.

Ingredients (for 4 people)

- 500 g fresh spinach or the equivalent frozen
- 150 g weight onion and/or spring onions, chopped
- 1 large leek, washed and chopped (optional)
- 2 garlic cloves, crushed
- 200 g *féta* or *beyaz* cheese
- 1.5 tsp dried dill or 2 tbsp fresh, chopped
- 1.5 tsp dried parsley or 2 tbsp fresh (flat-leaved), chopped
- 75 ml olive oil
- salt & pepper

*For the pastry*

- 400 g filo, 450 g puff or 425 g shortcrust (ready rolled sheets are ideal) — or try *yufka!*

Preheat the oven to 180° C. Wash the spinach well, dry it, and trim the thick stem parts off the spinach leaves. Then cut the spinach into shreds.

Heat the oil in a frying pan and cook the onion, garlic, spring onions (and leek, if used) until soft. Add the herbs, then the spinach, and toss the mixture until the spinach wilts and excess moisture evaporates. Stir in the *féta* or *beyaz* and add pepper and salt to taste — remembering that the cheese will be fairly salty. (Lancashire creamy or crumbly cheese and similar cheeses make good substitutes for *féta*. Eileen has even used a mix of crumbled cheese and grated cheddar which worked well.)

Prepare a 26 cm x 20 cm oblong dish or tin (like a large lasagne dish) or 20 cm round dish or tin by oiling lightly.

Roll out your pastry of choice, or butter and layer around 5 sheets of filo pastry, and line the dish or tin.

Fill with the spinach and cheese mixture, then cover with another layer of pastry or filo, sealing the edges. Make slits in the top to allow steam to escape, and brush with egg or milk. Sesame seeds can be also scattered over the crust before baking. Bake for around 30min, until the pastry is golden brown.

Serve either hot or cold. This goes well with mashed potatoes and tinned baked beans. *Ispanak böreği* also goes really well with potatoes and carrots mashed together. Cook the potatoes and diced carrots in the same pan (helpful when self- catering, where space and pans are at a premium) for 20min, then mash together with some pepper (great as a topping for other dishes like shepherd's pie).

*Alternative:* Make pasties using the same mixture. Roll out the pastry and, using a small plate as a guide, cut out circles. Put mixture on one half, moisten the edge, fold in half, seal and make a couple of small slits on top. Place on a baking sheet and cook as for the main dish, but only for around 15min.

## Brandy Sour

Brandy Sour is the national drink of Cyprus — thanks to King Farouk of Egypt. In his early days he liked to visit Cyprus and often stayed at the Ledra Palace Hotel, the only five star hotel on the island at the time. The monarch had a liking for Western-style cocktails, but wanted a drink not instantly recognised as alcoholic. The Brandy Sour was devised for him, and its popularity soon spread to the whole island.

Here is a typical recipé: sugar the rim of a glass, add a few ice cubes, pour in 50 ml Cypriot brandy, 25 ml Cypriot lemon cordial and 2-4 drops of Angostura bitters. Top with soda water (or lemonade for a slightly sweeter drink) and serve with a slice of fresh lemon.

An invigorating and undulating walk with views far along the Karpaz Peninsula. The goal is the impressively sited Kantara Castle at 630m/2067ft, seen from miles around. It is hard to imagine that this now sleepy corner was ever in the front line as protection from invaders — and where even Richard the Lionheart left his footprint.

# kantara circuit

# WALK 9

**Distance:** 8.7km/5.4mi; 2h50min (allow extra time for exploring the castle)

**Grade:** moderate, with some short steep sections beyond the castle; overall height gain of approximately 180m/590ft

**Equipment:** see page 22

**Transport:** 🚗 Head east towards Kaplica on the coast road (see map inset on pages 28-29). *Ignore* the first road off right to Kantara via Mersinlik (a scenic route, but very winding); continue to Kaplica. Turn left uphill through the village and onto a new road to Kantara village. Park in the open area by Kantara Restaurant.

**Refreshments:** Kantara Restaurant at Kantara or Kaplica Restaurant back down on the coast

**Shorter walk:** 7km/4.4mi; 2h20min. Just walk as far as the castle and return the same way; this avoids some of the steep but short uphill sections later in the walk.

**The walk starts** from **Kantara Restaurant**: follow the road signposted to Kantara Castle, meandering through light woodland decked with cyclamen in spring. The road traverses the mountainside with views south to the coast, eventually dipping past a large wooded **picnic area** on the right. Follow the road as it swings left uphill to **Kantara Castle** (**1h10min**); the track ahead here is the onward route.

After exploring the castle, or just enjoying this fantastic viewpoint, return downhill and go left along the track. As the track curves below the castle, a water pipe runs alongside the track, on the left, but the pipe goes off right just before the track bends left. There are great views now over the north coast and, on a clear day, even over to Turkey. Dipping below the castle, the main track sweeps downhill to the right in a U-bend (**1h30min**). At this point turn sharp left uphill onto a wide **fire-break** — with an excellent view towards the castle.

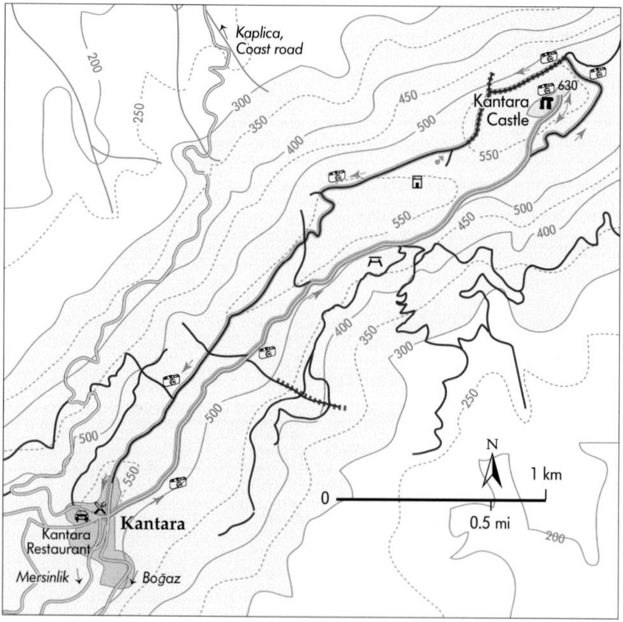


The ascent becomes steeper before, nearing the top, the route reverts to a track which levels briefly as it heads towards a white watchtower. This very pleasant pastoral track undulates along the contour. Ignore a track off left and stay ahead into a dip, with a **water point** on the left. Around 20 minutes later, where a grassy track goes right, stay on the main track as it sweeps left uphill (**2h10min**). You now have another short steep climb. Once at the top, swing right along the mountainside, leaving the **white tower** behind.

Continue on a switchback course in a south-westerly direction along the contour, ignoring tracks off left and right. Rise to sparsely-populated **Kantara village** — the houses are mainly abandoned or used as summer residences. From here descend back to the road you took to the castle (ahead is the road to Boğaz on the south coast). Turn right along your outward route, back to the start at **Kantara Restaurant** (**2h50min**).

Kantara Restaurant (see overleaf)

## Carob & *Pekmez*

The carob tree, *Ceratonia siliqua,* flourishes on Cyprus, producing long black pods in late summer. Since both the pods and the seed have important commercial uses, the carob industry brought wealth to the island over many generations. Although those days are past, old carob warehouses can still be seen along the harbour in Kyrenia and Famagusta.

The protein-rich seeds are used to make an edible gum widely used in the food industry in many products, from ice cream to jelly. After roasting and processing, the pods can be converted to a chocolate-like powder, used in bread-making, milk drinks or as a chocolate substitute.

In North Cyprus the whole bean still plays an important role — in the production of *pekmez,* a very versatile molasses-like syrup. You might find a dish of *pekmez* on your breakfast table to sprinkle over your cereal. It is loaded with trace elements, protein and some natural sugars, although it is not overly sweet. It is also used to flavour stews and other dishes.

# Kantara Grill and Fish Restaurant

A pleasant place for a drink, snack or meal — even taken outside in January sunshine. Most customers are en route to or from Kantara Castle, but it is also a popular destination restaurant with the locals on Sundays. Fish is available, especially on Sundays, when it's prepared for the locals.

**KANTARA**
**in the centre of Kantara ( (0392) 3882370 or (0533) 8436708/ 8656747**
**daily from 08.00 'till late' ££**
the basic menu offers **familiar fare** – snacks, **fish & chips**, ***kebaps*** (which come with ***mezes***).

Ask what they have *apart from* what's on the menu. They might have *hamsi,* fried small fish like whitebait; it's in season from November to February, but frozen otherwise.

*Hamsi* are easy to cope with if self-catering. When buying, the smaller the fish the better otherwise clean and bone but leave the tails. They are usually found in frozen food cabinets in supermarkets. These fish are eaten whole and go well with *rakı.* This method also works well at home with whitebait. Allow 200 g of small fish per person (if serving as a *meze,* the quantity will depend on how many other dishes are offered). See method opposite.

restaurants

eat

## *Ciğer* (Fried chicken livers)

Even those who say they do not like liver will find the chicken livers in North Cyprus melt in the mouth. This dish is quick and easy to prepare – ideal when self-catering.

Heat oil in a frying pan and prepare the liver by cutting off any bits of fat (usually very little), and then into bite size pieces.

Soften the onion in the pan, then add the liver and seasoning. Sauté a few minutes, then add the parsley (if using). Do not overcook. The liver is ready when it is still slightly pink inside but cooked.

Serve with rice (as shown here), mashed potatoes, or a mix of carrot and potato mashed, and perhaps broccoli.

<u>Ingredients (for 2 people)</u>

400 g chicken livers
1 tsp cumin or curry powder
1 onion, chopped
salt & black pepper to taste
1/2 bunch fresh parsley, finely chopped (optional)
oil for frying

## *Hamsi kızartması (photograph opposite)*

Heat vegetable (*not* olive) oil in a deep pan, filled to at least 5cm (1 inch), until very hot.

Wash and dry the fish and coat with seasoned flour, shaking off excess flour.

Fry the fish in the hot oil until brown, which won't take long. Drain on kitchen paper and serve with lemon quarters.

# 4

The Karpaz peninsula, that long finger of land extending out eastwards known sometimes as 'the panhandle', is the least spoilt part of Cyprus. Deserted beaches, wild donkeys, a scattering of small archaeological sites and early Christian churches lie in wait.

# the karpaz peninsula

# EXCURSION

**Distance:** 330km/205mi to the end of the peninsula and back – a long day's driving. Expect slow progress on the minor peninsula roads. An overnight stop is the ideal option if you want to explore in detail.

**Route:** Kyrenia – Geçitkale – Boğaz – Yenierenköy – Sipahi – Agia Triás – Agios Thyrsos – Dipkarpaz – Apóstolos Andréas – Zafer Burnu –Kyrenia

**Refreshments:** Vine Terrace, Deks, Alevkayalı

**Leave Kyrenia** by heading eastwards, passing by the villages of **Ozanköy** and **Çatalköy**. Where the road ahead leads inland over the Beşparmak Pass, turn left to join the **coast road** to Esentepe. Keep on the coast through a barren landscape rapidly filling up with villas. Ignore the turning to Esentepe and keep along the coast to reach a junction with a new road. Turn right here to head for Geçitkale. Although a new road, watch out for changes of level and a short unfinished section part-way along.

You will notice Geçitkale with its impressive mosque over to the right as you near the end of this road. The road ends at a T-junction with a petrol station on the left; turn left here. A steady run takes you now to the **Famagusta coast road**, where you turn left, passing through the small resort of **Boğaz** and starting along the **Karpaz Peninsula**.

Some 10km along turn off left to **Büyükkonak**, famed for its traditional craft centre and well worth this diversion. Then return and continue along the main road across the peninsula to the north coast. You pass a good restaurant on the left (Vine Terrace; see page 133) just before coming into **Yenierenköy**. This is the second-largest village on the peninsula and has a petrol station and tourist office. Yenierenköy, or 'New Erenköy',

This very unusual sandal mosaic at Agia Triás is the only one of its kind on Cyprus.

is a resettlement of residents from the original Erenköy, now just a Turkish army enclave in the Greek Cypriot sector. Like most of the Karpaz villages, it is a farming community. *Before* reaching the centre, take the right turn signposted to Sipahi. Drive via **Sipahi**, a predominantly Greek village, to find **Agia Triás** on the far side. The site is fenced, but the gates are usually left open for you to wander around this three-isled **5th-century basilica**. The **mosaics** here, although mainly geometric, are impressive — look for the very unusual sandal mosaic which is believed to symbolise pilgrimage; it is the only one of its kind on Cyprus.

Rejoin the coast road and turn right to continue. **Agios Thyrsos** and **Deks Restaurant** (see page 133) are reached very shortly. The church dates from the 18th century, but a much older, smaller **shrine** by the water's edge was served by a healing spring, hence the wish rags. Walk 10 starts here.

About 1km further along is **Alevkayalı**, an excellent fish restaurant (££-£££; ✆ (0533) 8760911; open daily 11.00 'till late'). It's very popular with the locals. The fish platter comes with a salad and a few *mezes*.

Very shortly remote **Dipkarpaz** is reached, the largest village on this under-populated peninsula. Following signs to Zafer Burnu/Monastir, the route switches over to the south coast, and

the chances of seeing **wild donkeys** increases from here to the end of the peninsula. These donkeys seem to have longer legs and longer ears than is usual. Watch out, too, for **Golden Beach**, which is slightly hidden in places by advancing sand dunes. This 5km-long gold sand beach is the finest the island can offer and one of several used by turtles for summer nesting.

The **Monastery of Apóstolos Andréas** is served by a dwindling, elderly Greek community which became isolated here after 1974, and a local priest. If the church is locked, one of the volunteers is usually around to unlock it (and will expect a small donation towards upkeep). While the present church is quite modern, there has been worship on this site since (according to legend) the Apostle Andrew found the ship on which he was returning to Jerusalem running out of fresh water. He went ashore here and summoned a spring. This fresh-water spring, reputedly with healing powers, is still by the sea. But serious mass pilgrimage only started in the early 20th century, when a woman's pilgrimage to the shrine led to the miraculous recovery of her son, kidnapped 17 years earlier. This once-secluded outpost now attracts a plethora of souvenir-sellers.

Just 4km further on, along a good stabilised track, is the ultimate turning point, **Zafer Burnu**, the 'Land's End' of Cyprus. Here you can stand at the most easterly point on the island and enjoy the absolute wilderness, before retracing your route back to Kyrenia.

10

The gently undulating terrain of the Karpaz Peninsula is the setting for this walk. Over the passage of time, an ever-changing population has left its mark, including some abandoned, enigmatic statues and the sites of looted Bronze Age tombs.

# puzzling statues of the karpaz

# WALK

**Distance:** 6.4km/4mi; 2h10min

**Grade:** easy track and path walk with minimal gradients, but an overall height gain of 142m/366ft

**Equipment:** see page 22

**Transport:** 🚗 From Yenierenköy on the Karpaz Peninsula (see map inset on pages 28-29) head east for about 7km, to the church of Agios Thyrsos on the shore side of the road, next to Deks Restaurant, and park.

**Refreshments:** Deks Café/Bar Restaurant and, 1km further east, Alevkayalı Restaurant; also the Vine Terrace Restaurant near Yenierenköy

**Start the walk** at **Agios Thyrsos**: cross the road from the church and head inland on the track opposite. Skirting a gully on the left, you reach a track junction after 600m. Turn right and, at the junction which follows immediately, go left along a gently rising track, into an area of low rocky hills. At a fork, stay left and, 300m further on, take a stony short-cut track up left (**25min**). (Or stay on the main track and keep left at a fork — slightly longer, but easier.)

Having taken the short-cut, turn left when you meet the main track again, to continue rising. The track bears right, as a valley drops away to the left. Keep ahead on the main track and ignore tracks off left. The **rocky outcrop** seen on the hillside ahead is near the abandoned statues and may have been the site of an **ancient quarry**. Turn left at a T-junction (**red blob waymarks**), and soon reach a multiple track junction. The second track on the left is the return route, but first find the statues which are to the right; **blue arrows and red waymarks** lead the way. Just continue to the right, off the track, on the second of two paths (the one nearest the stone field boundary now over to your left).

The waymarks lead you straight to the spot amongst olive

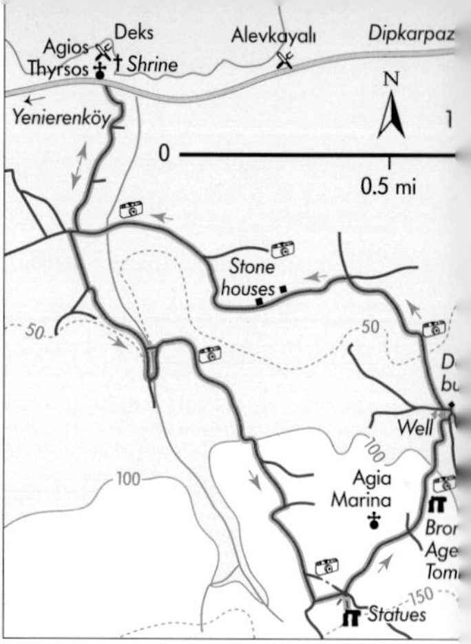


and carob trees where the **statues** are lying. One, a female, is now lying on her back, but was once probably attached to the plinth at her feet. Close by is that of a larger male lying on his side. The statues remind us of larger 6th-century BC statues of Kouros on Naxos in the Cyclades, which were broken and abandoned in an ancient marble quarry.

Return to the track junction (**1h**) and continue ahead towards the coast. Notice the Greek church of Agia Marina ahead, obscured initially by a tree. Relax into a very pleasant walk past carob trees and **Agia Marina** across the field to the left. Ignore a vague crossing track at the point where the main track becomes more of a field track and passes an area of **Bronze Age tombs** on the right. Views open out seawards as the track begins a stony descent.

At a T-junction opposite a **derelict stone building**, turn left (there is a **well** on the left here). Immediately, follow the main track downhill to the right; do *not* go straight ahead. Just keep heading downhill to the plain, where the track swings left and winds along parallel with the shore. Stay in the same direction, passing **two stone houses** on the right. When you rejoin your outward route (**2h**), turn right, back to **Agios Thyrsos** (**2h10min**). Don't miss the tiny shrine on the shore below Deks; it once housed a healing spring and is a magnate for pilgrims.

# Deks Bar-Restaurant

Perched on the cliff edge in an excellent position, next to the 18th century church of Agios Thyrsos (open). An older shrine, still a destination for pilgrims (even though the healing spring in its crypt has long-since ceased to flow) is tucked into the cliff on the shore below Deks.

Relaxing at Deks

**DEKS BAR-RESTAURANT**
**by Agios Thyrsos church ☎ (0533) 8309568; daily, 12.00-23.00 ££**

**light snacks** like toasted sandwiches, baked potatoes, egg & chips, hot & cold *mezes*

more **substantial fare** – various chicken dishes, **fish** (mussels, marlin steaks)

**desserts** – and even hot chocolate

# Vine Terrace Restaurant

In a pleasant setting and with a Cypriot atmosphere. Diners in warm weather can choose to sit on the covered, open terrace or in the garden. The menu is varied and the food good.

**VINE TERRACE**
**just west of Yenierenköy, on the sea side of the coast road, signposted ☎ (0392) 3744778/(0542) 8548034 daily, for lunch and dinner ££**

**light snacks**; **mezes**, ***kebaps***

**fresh fish**, pork chops

**Cypriot desserts**

## *Köfte* (Meatballs)

Mix all the ingredients thoroughly for a few minutes but add the egg gradually as the mix needs to be firm, not sloppy. Divide into 16 table-tennis size balls and coat lightly with the flour.

Heat 1 cm (1/2 inch) depth sunflower or rapeseed oil in a frying pan. Cook the meatballs over a medium heat until they are brown all over and just cooked, but moist in the centre.

Drain on kitchen paper and serve with salad or mashed potatoes or chips — or in a rich bean soup as shown here.

Ingredients (for 4 people)

500 g lean minced beef
1 medium onion, grated
1/2 tsp dried oregano
1/2 tsp dried mint
1 tsp dried parsley or 2 tbsp of finely chopped fresh
1 tbsp red wine (optional)
1 thick slice of white bread, dunked in cold water (squeeze out the water and remove the crust)
1 small egg
salt & black pepper
3 tbsp flour for coating

## *Kalamar* (Fried Squid)

Allow 250 g squid per person; you can use fresh or frozen. Wash the squid, then dry thoroughly. The tentacles will be separate, but leave the small squid whole and cut large fish into rings. All that is needed is to coat them in peppered flour and fry in hot fat, about 3min, until brown and crispy. *Overcooking toughens the flesh.* Drain on kitchen paper. Serve with lemon wedges.

Fried cuttlefish and squid

## *Çoban salatası* (Shepherd's salad; *not illustrated*)

This popular Cypriot salad, which is often found in supermarkets, does not normally include lettuce. Our recipe can be varied, to include olives and cheese.

Toss all the ingredients for the salad together. To make the dressing, put the lemon juice, oil and seasoning in a screw-top jar and shake well. Pour over the salad just before serving.

Great with fresh crusty bread.

Ingredients (for 4 people)

- 2 large tomatoes, chopped into small pieces
- 1 medium cucumber (more if they are small), chopped into small pieces
- 1 medium sweet red onion, chopped
- 1 green or red pepper (not the hot variety), chopped
- 1 small spring onion, chopped
- 1/2 bunch fresh parsley, finely chopped
- Salt & black pepper
- 1/2 lettuce, finely shredded (optional)
- 6-8 black or green olives, chopped (optional)
- 125 g *helim, beyaz peynir* or féta — or any mild, white crumbly cheese, cubed or crumbled (optional)

*For the dressing*

- 1 to 1-1/2 lemons (juice of)
- 3-4 tbsp olive oil
- salt & black pepper

Cheese-making in North Cyprus: straining *beyaz peynir* in baskets (above); pressing *helim* under bricks (left)

11

This city walk describes a circuit around Nicosia taking you to all the major points of interest and through areas where you might not venture without the blue line to guide you. All you need to do is follow the broad blue line painted on the road.

# nicosia blue line trail

# WALK

The timing for this walk is up to you. If you get hung up along the shopping street, or become absorbed by the many points of interest, or if you stop for lunch, then you can count on four hours or more, so plan to make a day of it.

The places which drew our attention especially were the **social housing** (not numbered on the trail map, but in the Samanbahçe Zone, between trail points 19 and 1). The **Mevlevi Museum**, trail point 20, was good for an insight into the Whirling Dervishes — it was an actual lodge for the Dervishes but closed in 1954. The Whirling Dervishes do visit once or twice a year for prayer. We were fortunate to observe them in their whirling prayer ceremony which must be done in absolute silence and without clapping.

**St Luke's Church** (again, not numbered, but passed on

**Distance:** 4.5km/2.8mi; 2-4 hours

**Grade:** easy city walk

**Equipment:** see page 22

**Transport:** 🚌 or 🚗 to Nicosia (see map on pages 28-29), then use the map on the inside front cover

**Refreshments:** see page 128

**Note:** You can join the blue line walk anywhere, but make sure you follow the shortest route to Kyrenia Gate Tourist Office, where you can pick up the Nicosia Trail map. The map numbers the places of interest with photographs and brief background information on the reverse side. The route is also well punctuated with information boards which help to confirm your location.

Make for Kyrenia Gate early on — it houses the Tourist Office

the way from trail point 1 to point 2), is now a restoration workshop for the craft shop found down the road opposite point 6. We just wandered in to inspect the church but found a workshop

Whirling Dervishes at the Mevlevi Museum (left), typical shop (below) and social housing (bottom left)

instead. The workmen were delighted to show us around and inspect the ornate chest they were busy restoring.

Other highlights for us included the **Buyuk Han**, **Selimiye Mosque** and the **Arasta shopping street**.

Ledra Street leaves from the end of Arasta street, so turning down here will lead you to a crossing point into the Greek Cypriot sector of Nicosia but you will need your passport (and some euros).

There are plenty of places to eat in Nicosia, but for some truly Turkish Cypriot food try **Müze Dostleri** (£-££), by the side of Selimiye Mosque. There is a chalked menu board outside which is changed daily. If you are not sure what is on offer just go into the kitchen. Rich bean soup seems to be a regular dish, sometimes with *köfte* (meat balls; see page 134) or even the *molohiya* speciality (see page 70). For more of a restaurant atmosphere, **Boghjalian Mansion Restaurant** (££; closed Sundays) on Salahi Pevket Street (between trail points 17 and 18) is a quiet oasis. The food here is fairly traditional, with a good selection of *meze* starters on offer, and chicken and *meat* main dishes.

Müze Dostleri (above) and the Boghjalian Mansion (left)

Although English is widely spoken in North Cyprus, a good phrase book can be helpful. It is particularly useful to learn the basic rules of pronunciation (there are only around six or seven), so that you can at least pronounce the names of places and food almost correctly. This can be done quite easily in just a few moments. Master these simple rules and you are a good way towards pronouncing Turkish words.

c is pronounced like 'j'. Example: Ercan, the airport, is pronounced 'Erjan'.

ç becomes 'ch'. Example: Koruçam sounds like 'Korucham'.

ğ is silent, but elongates the preceding vowel. Example dağ (mountain) sounds like 'daah'. Sometimes it introduces a slight y sound when it makes the word easier to pronounce: Gazimağusa sounds like 'Gazimaayusa'.

ı the undotted i, which can be lower case or capitalised, makes an 'uh' sound. Example: *rakı* is pronounced 'rakuh'.

ö sound sounds like 'ur'. Example: sörf (surf) sounds like 'surf'.

ş is pronounced as 'sh'. Example: şarap (wine) sounds like sharap.

ü is pronounced as in 'few'. Example: süt (milk) sounds like 'suit'.

**MENU ITEMS**

*ahtapot:* octopus
*aşure:* a sweet of grains, nuts and fruits (Noah's pudding)
*ayran:* yoghurt drink
*balık:* fish
*bamya:* okra
*barbunya:* mullet (usually red mullet)
*biber:* pepper
  *karabiber:* black pepper
*biftek:* steak
*bira:* beer
*bonfile:* sirloin
*cacık:* yoghurt, cucumber, & garlic dip
*çay:* tea
*ciğer:* liver
*çips:* crisps
*çorba:* soup
*çorban salatası:* simple mixed salad
*deniz ürünü:* seafood

# GLOSSARY

*dolma:* vine leaves rolled and stuffed with mince and rice
*domates:* tomato
*domuz:* pork
*dondurma:* ice cream
*ekmek:* bread
*elma:* apple
*fasulye:* bean
*bakla:* broad bean
*fileto:* filet
*havuç salatası:* carrot salad *meze* (par boiled, grated carrot with yoghurt and garlic)
*hindi:* turkey
*humus:* purée of chickpeas
*imam bayıldı:* aubergine shoe filled with tomatoes and onion
*kabak:* courgette
*kabuklular:* shell fish
*kahve:* coffee
*kalamar:* squid
*karides:* prawn
*kavaltı:* breakfast
*kavun:* melon
*kayısı:* apricot
*kiliç balığı:* swordfish
*kısır:* bulgar wheat salad
*kızarmış patates* chips (French fries)
*kuzu:* lamb
*lahmacun:* 'pizza'
*levrek:* sea bass
*limon:* lemon
*makarna:* pasta
*manti:* Turkish pasta
*meyve:* fruit
*mezgit:* hake
*muz:* banana
*omlet:* omelette
*pancar:* beetroot
*patatas:* potatoes
*patatas salatası:* potato salad
*patlıcan:* aubergine
*peynir:* cheese
*beyaz peynir:* white cheese
*mavi peynir:* blue cheese
*piliç:* young chicken (*tavuk:* hen)
*pirinç:* rice
*pirzola:* chops (usually lamb)
*rakı:* strong alcoholic drink, aniseed flavoured
*ringa yavrusu:* whitebait
*Rus salatası:* Russian salad
*salata sosu:* salad dressing
*salatalık:* cucumber
*sarımsak:* garlic
*sebze(ler):* vegetable(s)
*som balığı:* salmon
*su:* water
*süt danası:* veal
*sütlaç:* rice pudding
*suyu:* juice
*meyve suyu:* fruit juice:
*şarap:* wine
*beyaz şarap:* white wine
*kırmızı şarap:* red wine
*şiş:* spit or skewer
*şiş kebap:* meat cooked on a skewer
*balık şiş:* fish cooked on a skewer
*tavşan:* rabbit
*taze:* fresh
*tereyağı:* butter
*ton balığı:* tuna
*tuz:* salt
*üzüm(ler):* grape(s)
*yağ:* oil
*yenibahar:* allspice
*yumurta(lar):* egg(s)
*zeytin:* olive
*siyah zeytin:* black olive
*yeşil zeytin:* green olive
*zetin yağı:* olive oil

**SHOPPING TERMS**

bottle: *şişe*
kilo: *kilo*
half kilo: *yarım kılo*
carrier bag: *naylon torba*
allspice: *yenibahar*
apples: *elma*
apricot: *kayısı*
aubergine: *patlıcan*
bananas: *muzler*
basil: *fesleğen*
bay leaf: *defne yaprağı*
beans, french: *fasulye*
beans, broad: *bakla*
beef: *et or sığır eti*
beer: *bira*
bread: *ekmek*
bread (olive): *zeytin ekmek*
butter: *tereyağı*
cabbage: *lahana*
cake: *pasta*
carrots: *havuç*
cheese: *peynir*
cherries: *kiraz*
chestnut: *kestane*
chicken: *piliç* or *tavuk* (hen)
breast fillets: *göğüs filet*
breast pieces: *göğüs şiş*
drumsticks: *but baget*
legs: *kalça*
mince: *piliç kiyma*
thighs: *but talenks*
wings: *kanat*
chickpeas: *nohut*
chocolate: *çikolata*
chop: *pirzola*
cinnamon: *gemahlener zimt*
coffee: *kahve*

courgettes: *kabak*
cream: *krema*
cucumber: *salatalık*
cutlets: *pirzola* or *külbasti*
egg(s): ***yumurta(lar)***
fillet: *fileto*
fish: *balık*
cod, fresh: *morina*
sea bass: *levrek*
swordfish: *kılıç*
trout: *alabalık*
tuna: *ton balığı*
whitebait: *mezgit*
flour: *un*
fresh: *taze*
frozen: *donmuş*
fruit: *meyve*
garlic: *sarmısak*
grapes: *üzüm*
ham: *jambon*
honey: *bal*
ice: *buz*
cream: *dondurma*
jam: *reçel*
lamb: *kuzu*
lettuce: *marul*
liver: *ciğer*
margarine: *margarin*
meat: *et*
on a skewer for barbecuing: *şiş*
melon (water): *karpuz*
melon: *kavun*
milk: *süt*
mince: *kiyma*
mint: *nane*
mushrooms: *mantar*
mussels: *midye*
octopus: *ahtapot*
oil: *yağ*
olive: *zeytinyağı*
olives: *zeytin*
onions: *soğan*
oranges: *portacal*
oregano: *yabani mercan kösk*
parsley: *maydanoz*
pastry: *pasta*
peach: *şeftali*
peas: *bezelye*
pepper: *biber*
pork: *domuz eti*
potatoes: *patatas*
prawns or shrimps: *karides*
rice: *pirinç*
rosemary: *biberiye*
salad: *salata*
salt: *tuz*
sardines: *sardalye*
sausage: *sosis*
seafood: *deniz ürüleri*
soup: *çorba*
spaghetti: *makarna/spageti*
spinach: *ıspanak*
squid: *kalamar*
sugar: *şeker*
strawberries: *çilek*
tea: *çay*
tomatoes: *domates*
veal: *dana*
vegetables: *sebze*
vinegar: *sirke*
walnuts: *ceviz*
water: *su*
wine: *şarap*
white: *beyaz*
red: *kırmızı*
rosé: *pembe*
yoghurt: *yoğurt*

## CONVERSION TABLES

**Weights**

| | |
|---|---|
| 10 g | 1/2 oz |
| 25 g | 1 oz |
| 50 g | 2 oz |
| 110 g | 4 oz |
| 200 g | 7 oz |
| 350 g | 12 oz |
| 450 g | 1 lb |
| 700 g | 1 lb 8 oz |
| 900 g | 2 lb |
| 1.35 g | 3 lb |

**Volume**

| | |
|---|---|
| 15 ml | 1 tbsp |
| 55 ml | 2 fl oz |
| 75 ml | 3 fl oz |
| 150 ml | 1/4 pt |
| 275 ml | 1/2 pt |
| 570 ml | 1 pt |
| 1 l | 1-3/4 pt |
| 1.5 l | 2-1/2 pt |

**Oven temperatures**

| °C | °F | gas mark |
|---|---|---|
| 140°C | 275°F | 1 |
| 150°C | 300°F | 2 |
| 170°C | 325°F | 3 |
| 180°C | 350°F | 4 |
| 190°C | 375°F | 5 |
| 200°C | 400°F | 6 |
| 220°C | 425°F | 7 |
| 230°C | 430°F | 8 |
| 240°C | 475°F | 9 |

***bold type:*** photograph; *italic type:* map



INDEX

First edition  published by Sunflower Books
PO Box 36061, London SW7 3WS • www.sunflowerbooks.co.uk



ISBN 978-1-85691-371-3

*Cover photograph:* Folk dancing at Bellapais Abbey
Photographs: the authors
Maps: Sunflower Books
A CIP catalogue record for this book is available from the British Library.
Printed and bound in China by WKT Company Ltd

## Acknowledgements

Many people helped in small ways with suggestions, recipes or hints on the Turkish language (Hatıce Kerımgil), and we thank them all. In particular we would like to acknowledge Sabri (Steve) Abit of Bellapais Gardens Hotel for his kindness, Pegasus Airlines (www.flypgs.com/en) for help with flights from Stansted to Ercan and Monarch Airlines (www.flymonarch.co.uk) for making our journey from Manchester to Larnaca more comfortable with leg room seats. As always, thanks to our dear editor, Pat Underwood, for driving us on!

**Before you go ...**
log on to
**www.sunflowerbooks.co.uk**
and click on '**updates**', to see if we have been notified of any changes to the routes or restaurants.

**When you return ...**
do let us know if any routes have changed because of road-building, storm damage or the like. Have any of our restaurants closed — or any new ones opened *on the route of the walk?* (Not city restaurants, please; these books are not intended to be complete restaurant guides!)

Send your comments to mail@sunflowerbooks.co.uk